RISE OF A KILLAH

RISE OF A KILLAH

GHOSTFACE KILLAH

ST. MARTIN'S PRESS
NEW YORK

The names and identifying characteristics of some persons described in this book have been changed, as have dates, places, and other details of events depicted in the book.

First published in the United States by St. Martin's Press, an imprint of St. Martin's Publishing Group

RISE OF A KILLAH. Copyright © 2024 by Dennis Coles. All rights reserved. Printed in Germany. For information, address St. Martin's Publishing Group, 120 Broadway, New York, NY 10271.

www.stmartins.com

Conceptualized by Domingo Neris, Jr. and transcribed by John Helfers for DNES Marketing
Production: Ellen Scordato for Stonesong
Interior Book Design: Stan Madaloni for studio2pt0, llc

ISBN 978-1-250-27427-4 (hardcover)
ISBN 978-1-250-27428-1 (ebook)

Our books may be purchased in bulk for promotional, educational, or business use. Please contact your local bookseller or the Macmillan Corporate and Premium Sales Department at 1-800-221-7945, extension 5442, or by email at MacmillanSpecialMarkets@macmillan.com.

First Edition: 2024

10 9 8 7 6 5 4 3 2 1

In Loving Memory of
Dianne L. Cunningham
April 3, 1952
June 28, 2013

Meislohn-Silvie Funeral Home, Inc.

All Praises Due to the Most High

TABLE OF CONTENTS

CHAPTER 1: ALL THAT I GOT IS YOU 8
CHAPTER 2: POISONOUS DARTS 18
CHAPTER 3: APOLLO KIDS 39
CHAPTER 4: CAN IT ALL BE SO SIMPLE .. 50
CHAPTER 5: PROTECT YA NECK 62
CHAPTER 6: RAINY DAYZ 80
CHAPTER 7: RISE OF THE IRONMAN 88
CHAPTER 8: ONE 104
CHAPTER 9: WU-TANG FOREVER 115
CHAPTER 10: SUPREME CLIENTELE 144
CHAPTER 11: DEF JAM...RUN 156
CHAPTER 12: MONEY COMES FIRST 171
CHAPTER 13: BLACK JESUS 193
CHAPTER 14: MALCOLM 210
CHAPTER 15: TRIUMPH 218

RISE OF A KILLAH

CHAPTER 1

ALL THAT I GOT IS YOU

Yeah, ohh yeah, this goes out
to all the families that went through the struggle
(All that I got is you)
Yeah, from the heart
(And I'm so thankful I made it through)
It was from the heart, everything was real

Yo, dwellin' in the past, flashbacks when I was young
Whoever thought I'd have a baby girl and three sons
I'm goin' through this difficult stage I find it hard to believe
Why my old Earth had so many seeds
But she's an old woman, and due to me I respect that
I saw life for what it's really worth and took a step back
Family ain't family no more, we used to play ball
Eggs after school, eat grits cause we was poor
Grab the pliers for the channel, fix the hanger on the TV
Rockin' each other's pants to school wasn't easy
We survived winters, snotty nosed with no coats
We kept it real, but the older brother still had jokes

Sadly, Daddy left me at the age of six
I didn't know nuttin' but Mommy neatly packed his shit
She cried, and Grandma held the family down
I guess Mommy wasn't strong enough, she just went down
Check it, fifteen of us in a three bedroom apartment
Roaches everywhere, cousins and aunts was there
Four in the bed, two at the foot, two at the head
I didn't like to sleep with Jon-Jon he peed the bed
Seven o'clock, pluckin' roaches out the cereal box
Some shared the same spoon, watchin' Saturday cartoons
Sugar water was our thing, every meal was no thrill
In the summer, free lunch held us down like steel
And there was days I had to go to Tech's house with a note
Stating "Gloria can I borrow some food, I'm dead broke"
So embarrassin' I couldn't stand to knock on they door
My friends might be laughin', I spent stamps in stores
Mommy where's the toilet paper, use the newspaper
Look Ms. Rose gave us a couch, she's the neighbor
Things was deep, my whole youth was sharper than cleats
Two brothers with muscular dystrophy, it killed me
But I remember this, mom's would lick her finger tips
To wipe the cold out my eye before school wit her spit
Case worker had her runnin' back to face to face
I caught a case, housin' tried to throw us out of our place
Sometimes I look up at the stars and analyze the sky
And ask myself was I meant to be here . . . why?

I was born in the projects in West Brighton. 780 Henderson. Apartment 7C, I think it was. My mother used to always talk about that place. I lived there until I was nine or ten. It was beautiful there. Just about my whole family was there. My grandmother lived in 3C, right below us. My grandmother on my mother's side, so her mother lived downstairs on the third floor.

I was a good kid growing up. Even growing up in the projects, I was innocent. I wasn't a bad kid, I didn't do a bunch of stupid stuff when I was growing up. I was cool. I never gave my mother no problem when I was young.

> "Hell, my mother was young when she had me, she was only around eighteen or so. My father was around the same age as her. He was an electrician, as I remember."

Life was simple back then. At least for me it was simple, it wasn't too hard, I had my aunts downstairs and all that. I didn't really know too much. I just know I loved my grandmother because I used to always go down to her apartment, and even my aunt's children, we all used to be down there, and we used to see who was going to go sit next to Grandma because we loved Grandma. We loved her too, too, too much. We called her Nana. She had little, flabby arms and we would go over there and just be like, "Yo, go grab her arms," and hold them just for a long time like we never wanted to let her go.

Whoever got up to go to the bathroom would lose their seat, and when they came back they'd start crying because they'd want to sit next to Grandma. Grandma was funny. But I remember one day I told my grandmother—to this day, I don't know what made me say this—I said, "Grandma, if you ever die, I'm going to drink a whole bottle of pine." Because she always kept pine (Pine-Sol) in the house to clean up. I think it was Pine-Sol because it was brown inside. But it was the old bottle, I don't even know if they sell them anymore. And I knew because they always would say like, "Don't drink that pine." That's how I knew I could say that because they always told kids like, "Yo, this is what to stay away from." So it had to be bad for you.

Sitting next to her like that, I can only guess that I said that because I loved her so much, and couldn't imagine being without her. I can't even remember her reaction. Because she used to watch the stories. You know grandmothers always watched stories all day, like *All My Children* and *As the World Turns*, *Young and the Restless*, and then go into *Price Is Right*. That's why I respect Bob Barker, because that motherfucker was there for decades. All the grandmothers was all about Bob Barker. I'm sitting next to her holding her arm watching all these little programs, *Adam-12*, *All in the Family*, all that. She had programs on every night.

When she did pass away, it was sad for all of us, especially me. I was somewhere around six or seven years old. I couldn't understand why Nana's face was so cold. They didn't tell me what had happened, but when I kissed her, she was cold, and I really didn't understand it. I was crying when I saw her, I just wanted her to come home. "Just come on. Just get up. Come on, just go. Come on, come on." Then you had to get used to her not coming home no more.

It was the '70s, it was a lot more beautiful, more at ease, more at peace. Sure, you had your drama over there in those places and stuff like that, but at the time we didn't have to worry about gunshots and all that. If there was a fight, it was more likely we were doing it with hands, no guns.

I was too young to be involved in any of that. You might hear about somebody getting shot. Certain names you remember, like, "Oh shit. Yo, this one got killed last night, and this one got killed." Remember I'm young, so I'm not staying out past a certain time. I'm hearing it secondhand from my cousins. It was like, "Yo, this one got shot or this one had a fight with this one." Back then it was like, "Okay, yeah, somebody got killed." It was like, "Oh shit." The projects were the projects. It might have been less pissy elevators and all that, but they were still the projects.

That's where I first started hearing hip hop, in West Brighton. DJ Jones and Dr. Freak used to bring the turntables out in front of the buildings, and at night they would DJ. Like how Kool Herc and them was doing up in the Bronx. But I remember them coming out like that, bringing the music out and everybody just outside, but I can't be down there because I'm too young. I got to look out the window. From the seventh-floor window. It was nice. It was great beats. It was a lot of old James Brown records and all that being cut up, "Good Times" by Chic, listening to the DJ just cut it up. It was amazing. It was amazing just hearing them and shit like that, and people gathering around to listen and dance in the street.

I also listened to a lot of old music because my mother used to bring her friends to the house when my father was at work. She would have her friends over, and they'd be listening to the Chi-Lites, Bloodstone, Stylistics, Isley Brothers, Marvin Gaye, New Birth, Rose Royce, and all that. So that was giving me my soul because I heard it repeatedly. I was inspired by the greats. But I had to go into another room and close the door and stay there because they kicked me out the living room because they were doing grown folks' stuff. Whether smoking weed or doing whatever they were doing. And I remember album covers laying around, and everything was getting played there, and that right there went into my body, into my soul. I carried that. That's why in the beginning you hear me rhyming off a lot of old soul because I'd rather rhyme off that than any new music because I felt that music, it was in my bones already. It really resonated with me. And my mother was indirectly responsible, because that's what she listened to, and that's what I grew up listening to, so I kind of took it on myself once I started writing and rhyming.

Then my father would come home and kick everybody out because he wasn't into that, a lot of people in the house, smoking and drinking and shit like that.

He was a good father during those early years. I can't really shit on him. At that time, he was good, I can honestly say that. But you know with parents, a lot of the times you don't know who was in the right, and who was in the wrong. Because the baby's mother could be like,

"Okay, your father ain't shit and he's not supporting us and whatever whatever," but it was probably a reason why he left. Or it could have been vice versa. But at that time, it was me and my two younger brothers, Devon and Darius, and my mother and my father, all up on the seventh floor. And he was a good father, he was there and everything. But then things spun to the left. It's like neither one of them could take it anymore, and one of them had to bounce. And that was it.

I'm not really sure when that was. I might've been around five or six years old. Anyway, one day he up and walks out the door, leaving my mother with me and my two brothers, Devon and Darius, both of whom have muscular dystrophy. That was another thing I was just aware of growing up. I remember stitches on the back of Devon's leg, the scar left there from an operation. I didn't ask about it because when you're young, you don't really ask questions, you just see stuff. You just go on with your life. But I knew Devon had muscular dystrophy because I would hear the term around the house. He used to be falling, he would walk, and he would fall, walk and fall, next thing he had to go to a walker, then to a wheelchair. And that's what happened to both of my brothers.

We got along without my father, but I didn't know the details of how my mother was surviving because I was too young. I really don't know because I didn't know about public assistance back then. Were my parents getting public assistance and all that? I didn't know. I'd heard them arguing. When you're that young, you kind of figure out something is wrong, but you don't know the true details of what's really going on.

I do remember one time something happened where my father had picked up my brother the wrong way, and his arm broke, or his collarbone broke or something like that. But he was little. Then I remember one time, they took me away. I remember they put me in handcuffs. I was a little dude. I remember that because I was going crazy. You taking me away from my family? Motherfucking police put me in the back of the fucking cop car and took me wherever they took me to. Then other people came and got me. They took me away again, and I wound up at some other white people's crib. It was on Staten Island, though. I think it was this white lady named Alice. I think they might have housed kids that got removed from their homes. Because I saw some other Black kids over there, too.

I'm not sure what caused that whole event. I never asked my father; it could have been the truth, it could have could have been a lie. I don't know. But he said one day he picked my brother up and his arm or collarbone got broke. That's it. My grandfather, my mother's father, watched me go into the fucking police car. It was just havoc. It was crazy. I didn't know where I was going. They just came and just snatched me up, like if I had a warrant or something. It was like, "Yo, what the hell?"

> "I want to make it clear that my father wasn't abusive to me or my brothers. Never ever, ever. It was never like he was beating the crap out of me and doing all this other stuff like that. Any beatings I got, I deserved because I did something or whatever and wasn't listening."

I remember my mother whipped my ass one day because I lost my sister. This would have been when I was around eight years old. I had my sister because she was small, too, and sometimes I would watch her. My mother said, "I'll be right back." Whatever. But then we're both outside the building, and I'm just watching my sister, and then I turned my head for a minute, and all of a sudden my sister walked off somewhere. That was scary.

One of the building's maintenance men brought her back. Oh, I got an ass whooping that day. You could hear that shit downstairs. My mother beat me. Not my father, my mother. Whipped my ass. I was scared to death.

I'm going to ask one of my mans about that when I see him next, too. Because I looked out the window after I got my ass beat and I was screaming so loud, I seen him looking up. Motherfucker's looking up at my window. I'm gonna ask him one day, "You remember that ass whipping I got?"

After a while we left the Henderson projects and lived in Stapleton for a couple years. A two-family house where we lived downstairs and another family lived upstairs. It was all my family, though. It was my stepfather's house, or possibly his mother's house. My third brother's father, his mother lived upstairs and all that. I guess my mother met him at my Aunt Marie's house over in the West Brighton projects. I still had cousins over there. Then, after they got acquainted and all that, that's when we moved to Targee Street, the street that, decades later, would become Wu-Tang Boulevard.

That's when the violence started coming. I saw it more hands-on. The drinking, and stuff like that. But you got to remember, my mother was still young. They're both young. You got to look at the parents back then. They're making young decisions, too. They were what, twenty-four years old? They're making a twenty-four-year-old's decision. She's not making a grown woman's decisions. She fell for the dude or they fell for each other. Then from there we moved into that house under his mother and his family. He'd get drunk, bugging out, doing his shit. But I told you when he was sober, he was a good dude.

He was good, but he was just wild. He was the wild one. He'd knock your block off. But he wasn't mean to the kids, though. But outside he wasn't nothing to fuck with. He might have been the roughest man. But he's good now. I think he's a preacher now or something like that. He's into the church now. But back then he used to drink a lot. When he wasn't drunk, he was cool. But my stepfathers, they were all alcoholics, drug addicts, whatever the case may be, except for my real father, who was the only one that had something going.

All the stepfathers did was add on to what my mother was doing already in terms of drugs or drinking or whatever. I guess that attracted that. Where they come in and fuck up your stuff. They were probably just living off her for a place to stay. Add to that the stress of both my brothers being in a wheelchair by this time. And I'm the oldest, so I got to do a lot of things myself. Take my brother, had to put him on the toilet by myself. I had to pick him up, pull his pants down, sit him on the toilet. After he's done his business, I had to pick him up, lift his pants up with the other hand, sit him back down, pick him up, put him in the wheelchair. I'm doing a grown man's job at like eleven, twelve, thirteen years old. That put the pressure on me. But I was the oldest, so whatever I got to do for my brothers, I got to do for them.

My mother took up with that shit for a year or two, I don't really know how long. Then we moved to the projects. We lived on the first floor. That apartment was legendary. My mother was one that'll take anybody in. Long as you had some money, you could pay your rent. That's one thing that I didn't really understand because she had a lot of drinking friends. But one of them bum ass niggas going to come off the street acting like he give you a check every month or whatever. A hundred dollars a month or two hundred. But as long as you're drinking with her and y'all paying the fucking money, you could get a bed in there.

That's why I said fifteen of us in a three-bedroom apartment. Cousins and aunts were there. Sleeping four to a bed. Roaches everywhere, in the kitchen cabinets, in our cereal boxes, when we were lucky enough to have some, just everywhere. That's what it was about. Because you have friends that get their little SSI checks or whatever, and they're crashing on the couches. Some of them shared the bedroom with us, me and my brother. Whatever the females was in there, they'd be in a room with my sister and them on a different bed.

The house was always crowded. If you came in too late, you couldn't even get in the fucking bed—you had to get in where you could fit in. The door was always open. Fuck around, and you might be downstairs, hanging around on the street outside and got to use the bathroom. "Yo, Diane, can I use your bathroom?" You come use the bathroom and just go back downstairs because we're right there. Right in front of the building. But we got services where you can just look off the building and stuff like that. That's how we let our people know where we lived at.

Stapleton looked like we could have been in jail. The fence is right there in front of you, you got eight floors with a fence there that you could just look over or you could look through it, and you could just see people outside.

We were so happy to be on the first floor. We saw everything. Like I said on "All That I Got Is You," when times were rough, I'd have to go borrow some milk or some sugar upstairs on the seventh floor from Ms. Gloria's apartment, and stuff like that. That's when I started going to the store with food stamps and all that. I'm doing a grown man's job at like fucking eleven or twelve years old. I'm doing all this at a young age. That put the pressure on me.

That right there catches you to start robbing and stealing because you wanted the latest fucking clothes, and you can't get them because you don't realize that your mother is on welfare and that welfare check don't pay that much. My brothers and I had to share the same clothes. He'd wear a pair of pants one day, I'd wear the other pair one day. Then he'd wear my pair the next day, and I'd wear his pants that day. At that time, we was away from our father. A lot of times we missed a few years from him with that, going and getting school clothes and all the shit like that until he had came back, until we got back in touch with him. I remember him buying me a few things during my junior high school years, but it was never enough.

CHAPTER 2

POISONOUS DARTS

What the fuck I got the moonshine, word to God let's get it on
Clap your heels three times, grab the magic wand
Nameless, these stonewashed cats leave him brainless
Showin' outta this world, stranded on Uranus
With coke and a dollar bill stems and crack capsules
Take a blast fool but we trap up crews it's natural
Like soybean, burn like a laser beam
My vaccine I shoot it firm and it connects like sideburns
The segment, rare fragment comes together
Like magnets, attract heads capture like Dragnet
Goin' through mad phases, of all ages
Killa beez locked the fuck up behind cages
The Genovese swallow this line and caught a freeze
Press call ID for me to quote more degrees
The fortune teller Tucker sleepin' gas umbrella
A war where they're gunnin' in the back of Armanbella
Now who, don't believe that cash must rule
I don't eat beef, I slap blood out of Purdue
Keep a Wallace mic, mics on strike the session
It's over, I file this and glow like fluorescent

Yo yo, methods of blow like snow constant cash flow
Rockin' a Shaft afro, Tony got mad glow
with hoes, mega powder drippin' from they nose
Fuckin' Jet magazine bitches with wild pussy pose
Send 'em for the whole night, daily venom horror snake bites
Only Built 4 Cuban Link Kings who shoot dice
Holdin' money that's convertible, beds with feathered bags
With the mongoose your man's got two seeds down in Baghdad
You onionhead niggaz spread out and parlay
Yo Rae these itch days get crashed with ash trays
I pull stings like, guitar strings down in Spain
I'm so hyped Jakes label God "crack cocaine"
Why Equality Self God, yeah yeah you know it kid
Ricki fucked up, and G-Pac, blow his wig
He's rocking Wu Wear, the latest in fleece uniform
He's a newborn, look at money swearin' like he's on
But anyway back to furry Kangols Jamaican wallabies
My back is on the wall, bombin' devils with trick-knowledgey
My heart is cold like Russia, got jerked at The Source awards
Next year two hundred niggaz comin' with swords!

One day in 1984 or '85, my friends came to school with hundred-dollar bills wrapped up and rings on their fingers and wearing Lees and all that, with me not knowing that these mothers had robbed someone. There was a car down there, they popped the hatchback open and picked up two bags and one had twenty-five thousand dollars in it. It was twenty-five Gs, and we were like thirteen or fourteen years old. And I'm thinking, "Damn." That became a big eye-opener because I was looking for that next vic like that.

I know now that there probably would never be another vic like that. But when you're young, you don't know. You're thinking you can just catch whatever. They had big leather gooses on, V gooses, radios. They're puffing all the weed they want. They're chilling. Leather jackets, pink leather Lees. All this other shit like that. That led me to start doing that. Doing all the other shit like that.

That's when I started transitioning to smoking weed, smoking dust, robbing and stealing. Because I wanted that lifestyle. Because I didn't have nothing. We grew up with shit. I remember my mom going to get that cheese. That welfare cheese. Come home with blocks with that shit. I used to come home from school, melt the grilled cheese sandwich, and eat that shit. I used to eat so much welfare cheese I got constipated. Then when we did get some food stamps, she would buy the cheapest fucking food. The no-frills kind. Damn, even the bag. All her bags were either green and black, black and white, or green and white, because that was the A&P kind. I used to feel bad. Like, "God damn, where's the colorful shit at? Where's the colors at, Mom?"

You don't know what your parents go through when they're struggling like that. She's trying to save as much money so she could smoke or drink it away. But as a kid, you don't recognize it. You could just see it, and shit like that. I kind of recognized a little bit because I was like, "Damn, I'm embarrassed. You're sending me to the store with these food stamps and you're going to send me up there with a note to go borrow some milk or some sugar from upstairs." Tell her, "Give her the money back this day or that day." I had to do that. I'm the oldest. All that pain fell on me without me even knowing. I remember my aunt used to come to the house and say, "You look depressed." You could be depressed without knowing you're depressed. All that shit is on my back. It's on my back.

As a young man, I wanted a life of my own. I wanted the nice things my friends had too, but I couldn't get them. That led me to, like I said, robbing and stealing. Snatching pocketbooks and shit. I'm over here snatching pocketbooks and robbing stores.

I remember the first real crime we did. I know we was just going around and breaking windows. Then I did a little grand theft shit. We would meet somewhere and might see some bridge tokens in there or some movies or a pocketbook in a car and smash the window. Snatch the pocketbook or whatever out of the car.

One day I just said . . . I was with my best friend one day and I just deboed the video store. The lady was behind the counter. I just said, "Fuck it." I just went back there and snatched like ten VHS tapes because we could sell them for ten dollars apiece. This dude, Mohammed, they used to buy them from us up in the hill. Up in Park Hill. Knock off the tapes. If we saw drills, power drivers, any type of tool, my friends knew where to get the tools off at. Then we'd go get high. We were smoking woolies around that time.

Me and my best friend Un were inseparable. Un . . . It's short for Understanding. But I'll let him tell ya . . .

Un and Ghostface

Un: Growing up, Ghost was living in the building behind mine. So it's a bunch of kids in the neighborhood. We had to be in our early teens. And we just was around each other constantly. We just started hanging out.

Ghostface: It's like God just put us together.

Un: You can't even pinpoint it. We can't even remember. It seems like ever since I was alive, I knew him. I really can't pinpoint it, but I know we was real young. What I do remember was that when we really started hanging out proper, we were just starting high school. Because I remember one day

21

when I was going to school and then I see Ghost in front of the building, he was in front of the building with them older dudes, right? And they was always up to no good.

So he was like, "Yo. Man, fuck the school, man. We going to go get this car and we going to sell the radio out the car and we going to get some money."

So I said, "You know something? You right." I threw the books away and I said, "Fuck the school. I'm going to get the money." We wound up stealing the car and all that. And then we go to Park Hill, about ten to fifteen minutes from our projects, walking. When they stole the car, me and Ghost was the youngest. There was two other dudes.

This is the part I remember. Back then, the crack cocaine was just really coming out. It was really just starting to be popular. All the older dudes that was with us, they sold the radio but, of course, they didn't give us no money. So we was just basically leeching on. But they went and bought crack, they went in the building and smoked it, and we just watched them. But the moral to that story is, every last one of them that smoked that crack became full-blown crackheads. So, as we was getting older, we used to see them messed up. Man. And we used to say, "Glad we didn't smoke that crack."

> "We was the first ones to actually do a carjacking in my projects. Because we used to smoke that red-devil business called PCP."

Ghostface: We was just young kids doing what young kids do. You know what I mean? We hung around the older guys and all that stuff like that. We learned from them. I said, "Yo, Park Hill was a bunch of fly niggas." Our project was really crooks and just fighters and all that other shit like that. What you see, you just out there doing what it do. You out there. You just pick up like little motherfuckers. You just pick up. You saw something you wanted. Yeah. Go ahead.

Un: We was also dealing with poverty at that time. So it was like our mothers couldn't keep their eye on us like that. We wasn't even in the house. We was outside doing all the wrong things at a young age and getting in all types of trouble.

I became a professional because I had a cousin who taught me how to do it. I would only steal Cutlasses... The car had to have tilt steering, which were mostly Cutlass Cieras. I was able to take it in less than three minutes. I was able to steal it fast. We used to steal a car, get the dust, ride back, and basically drive it all through the projects at about a hundred miles per hour. Cops be chasing us or whatever; always got away. I was always the driver and Ghost was the passenger. And he's sitting over there relaxed while I be driving. And you know what was crazy? We'd never even have fear. Nothing. We wasn't scared of crashing, we wasn't scared of nothing. We didn't care if we died or not. We just was looking like you either get some money and have some fun doing it. And that's how we did it.

There wasn't a crime we wouldn't do. Whatever we had opportunity to do, that's what we did. If we thought we could get it, we was going to get it. For instance, a friend of ours, his name was Jermaine, aka Big Den. So me and Ghost was just standing there, and he had a bomb. A bomb was at least a hundred crack vials or more, a lot of it. And when the police were chasing him, when the undercover cops were chasing him, he threw it over the fence. Me and Ghost was standing there where he threw it over the fence, so we seen what happened.

But it rained the day before, so the grassy part was muddy. So I said, "Ghost. Get the bomb." Ghost jumps over the fence, he gets the bomb and then we keep it. Now, when Big Den come back, he said, "Yo, I threw it over here." And we was like, "We ain't see it." He looked at Ghost's sneaker and it had all the mud on it. So he knew Ghost had it. He had all the mud on it, right? So from that incident on, we started beef with him and his crew. They was from a different building, so we started fighting them. But that's how we really got on. We got on from this guy throwing his bomb and we didn't care what he thought. We had the gun and whatever happened, happened... We stole that and got more money. We stole that and started going to buy our own crack.

Ghostface: I think we might have spent that and we fell off. And then, we started whacking. Remember, we whacked that dude for all the breadcrumbs.

Un: One day we thought we had it easy. It was a crackhead guy, but he wasn't always smoked out. He had a long trench coat on, right? We was trying to whack him or rob him for fifty dollars, take that fifty dollars off him.

So Ghost got to him first and had both his hands. But he got in the boxing stance, and he was just shooting the jabs at us—

Ghost: That nigga knocked me down. That nigga knocked me down three, four times. Straight jabs. Shit. His jabs. Yeah, I ain't going to front. He had a Tommy Hearns jab, because he was skinny and slim. But you know me, I'm coming like a young nigga thinking this, "All right. Yeah. Come on. We going to do it." And every time he stuck that jab out there, it just buckled me down. It's like, "Boom. Oh, shit. Get up." About two or three times, I went on my one knee and shit. Word, I can't front. And then, we had to get him. We both had to jump his ass after that shit.

Un: So we did all soaping, right? And this is one story I would never forget. We fucked around, and we knew a white boy. He had a motorcycle; he was a biker. So we sold him soap. We had sold him the fake crack in the projects, in the parking lot. But we on the bench, it's about 2:00, 3:00 in the morning. It's summertime. And we could see him coming through the projects on his motorcycle. He had a bat in his hand. And he came through trying to run us over there by 77. He tried to run us over. We had a long .38 gun. And this white guy wasn't scared of nothing, man. He wanted his money back, man. He didn't care about the bullets. He didn't care about the gun. And he was chasing us through the projects with that motorcycle. We was shooting at him and everything and this guy just wanted his money back. He wanted that crack. He can't get in the building, though. And after a couple of shots, he realized he had to get out of there, so he went away with nothing.

But this right here is what I'll never forget, too. My son was born, right? And a crackhead came selling Pampers. So Ghost got a cousin named Chandra and she had a best friend named Keeara. They getting under building 77. So when the crackhead came with the Pampers, I'm like, "Oh. Wow. My son could use that." But I said, "Yo, I'm gonna take the Pampers from him." Right? Anyway. So now, when the guy come with the Pampers, I take the Pampers and I hit him. He dropped everything, right? Ghost got the gun in his pocket. He's going in his pocket like he got a gun. So now, we running between 77 and 75. So now, Ghost thinking he got a gun so he trying to shoot him. Just missing me, though. You see what I'm saying? So he's chasing the guy and the guy's chasing like he got a gun. And Ghost is behind him shooting at him but just missing me. And the dude never had a gun. Never got the Pampers back.

It was a whole lot of incidents like that. We said, "Yo, we got to do something." And it's another incident when I thought Ghost was gonna shoot me, right? So this guy named Delmar Ramiro. We was in the projects called Mariners Harbor. We over there because now we selling a lot of drugs. Ghost was already part of the Wu at this point. So we come downstairs and Del's just talking.

So he said something slick to Ghost, I don't remember what. And then Ghost was like, "What?" And then Del was like, "Didn't you hear what I said?"

I knew where Ghost was going with it. He walked back in the building and got two guns, a 9mm and a .22. Now, me and him knew the 9mm had no bullets. But the .22 was loaded. So now when Del sees us come back downstairs, Ghost was coming with both guns. "Yeah, motherfucker. What you say? What you said?" I know him and he had the look, he had that blood in his eyes. He's like, "What the fuck you said?"

The dude, Delmar Ramiro, grabs me because he was a little older than us. He grabs me and he gives me the death grip. And he's trying to tell me to tell Ghost to stop. "Yo, get him. Get him."

So Ghost was like, "I'm not gonna shoot you." Ghost was going between my legs trying to shoot. Smacking him with the other gun, he was like, "Yo. Yo, come on. Get him. Get him." Ghost was trying to shoot him. This is the second time in my life I seen the devil in his eye, like, "This fucking guy."

I said, "Yo, you gonna shoot me."

He says, "I'm not gonna shoot you."

I said, "Chill. Chill." And when Del thought he ran out of bullets, he threw me and took off running.

Now, the irony of that story was Ghost got babies by Del's cousin. So they all pulled up in the van. And then they came down to Graham's house. He calls me. He calls me like, "Yo. Del and them's all downstairs. He got the whole family in the van, coming downstairs." But they had talked it out by then, so there was no more beef between them.

The other time I saw Ghost with blood in his eye, we was on a street called Gordon Street.

They had a little club over there, across from our projects, and we were going. So when we turned around, we see a cousin of mine named Chubby. He's fighting a dude. I forgot his name, we used to call him different names. He's fighting this dude, right? Now, we all circling them fighting. I got the gun and Ghost said, "Yo, what you doing, man? You just came away from getting out of trouble." And that's when I seen the motherfucking devil in his eye. And he clocked the guy. He clocked him right there.

Ghostface: I totally remember that, I remember they went to Jersey and got my chain snatched.

Un: Yeah. So then that was the time when I knew he was like, "Yo." So he clocked him and that was the first time.

After a while, we went to D.C. Let me tell you how we got there. I was messing with this girl named Lynne, and she had a friend. The Jamaicans was doing a lot of hustling back then. So her friend messed with this Jamaican guy and his name was Carl. And she realized me and Ghost were selling crack. Then she said, "Listen, I could put you on with my friend's boyfriend, Carl. He be going back and forth to Washington, D.C."

I said, "Yeah. Good." So I get Ghost. I said, "Yo, we could get some money in Washington, D.C." And that's how we started going out there, making the money out there. Now Carl already had the drugs out there, and we were supposed to sell it. But then, when we realized he wasn't paying us like he's supposed to pay us, then we just said, "Fuck Carl." And we started doing our own thing, again. And then that's when Ghost got into what he got into over there because I had to go back and see my probation officer.

Ghostface: My first trip out of state was to D.C., and that's where I got stabbed. Un took me out there with him, with this Jamaican dude, and everything was cool, and then Un had to go see his probation officer. He had to go see to that and I stayed there, and that night they set me up to get robbed. But I finished everything. I just had the money on me.

So this guy kept coming in and out of the room checking on me like, "Yo."

I'm like, "Yo, I'm dozing off." I'm like, "Yo." It was a theme. Like "Yo," he's asking me, "Yo, can I make it?" Man, I don't give a fuck what you make, ain't this your cousin's house? He kept coming in the room, sneaking in, waking me up—he was testing me. So I get him out, I hurriedly doze off.

> "And he came in there at night with a cup of bleach and just jumped on me. And when I got up, when I was on my back, so when I went to sit up, he threw the bleach in my face and blinded me. So we was fighting in the house. I grabbed that fucking knife and I broke it in half, boom, I broke the blade, bam."

I can't see. I can't see only very little bits. So me and him are fighting. Pushing him, fighting and boom, trying to get off this nigga so I can make it to the steps, so I can get out the door.

I fought my way up out of there like that. Now I'm by myself, because the dude that took me out there, he went back to New York because he took Un back to meet with his probation officer. So I'm by myself. I went across the street. It's pouring down, raining. I heard this nigga run out behind me and go somewhere and I'm just screaming. I'm in the middle of the rain, it's pouring, thundering out there. I'm drenched in water. I'm in the middle of the streets in Washington, D.C. I remember it was in Southeast D.C., and I'm screaming for help. But in the middle of the rain, shit was like a movie.

But I can just see a little bit, just a little tiny bit and I'm walking slow to the house that they brought me to earlier. But I made it there. I remembered the steps. I remembered the door where it was, but I still couldn't really see. I'm feeling around the walls. I'm doing this, feeling around, feeling around. Then I knock on the door and they opened up for me and they was like, "What the hell happened?"

They called the ambulance. I was in the paper the next day. They maintaining this and that, not knowing this nigga tried to rob me and stabbed me in my back. But I broke that fucking knife. I was so traumatized by everything that I was still clutching the broken blade in my bleeding hand.

Poisonous Darts

I was in the hospital for a minute. I had to get well, he took me, to his credit, he was mad. The dude that brought me out there, he was mad. I had to wait for both of my eyes to lighten because they was all red. They had to rinse both eyes out. Shit felt like I was drowning, that's torture, holding somebody's eyeballs open and just rinse them out. It feels like you drowning.

> "That was one episode that only a few people knew about, what I had to go through down there, because by the time I got back home, my eyes was cleared up for the most part."

Un: And listen, one thing about Ghost—he was tough on them broads, man. Females? He was tough on crime. So a female didn't give him back his money out in Washington, right. I want you to picture this. We were like, "Man, these fucking kids don't know what they really up against, I guess." Right? So Mark told us, "Listen, they about to do a raid, right. You all got to get out the house."

So I'm telling Ghost, "Yo, we got to get out of here." Right? But he seen the girl that he gave the crack to and she didn't give him his money. She wasn't a crackhead, though. But she had a nice jacket, she had earrings. So he's in the middle of the street and they about to do a raid. And I'm telling him, "Yo, come on, man. Fuck that. Let her keep it." He's in the middle of the street. Right? And don't you know what he does? He takes everything from this girl. He takes the earrings. He takes her jacket. He takes everything. He didn't care if the police was going to rush or not; he wanted his money from that girl. That's the type of personality he had. You wasn't going to get over on him.

We was walking around and it felt like death out there in D.C. It felt like death. At that time, I think they had the highest murder rate. But it's like we were going to the store and walked in, it just felt like death, like anything could happen. They looking at us, we just trying to keep an eye on those motherfuckers like, "Yo, shit seem real sneaky out here."

GHOST OF A CHANCE!

AN ILLUSTRATED RETELLING OF WHAT WENT DOWN IN D.C.

Once we left D.C., a bunch of Jamaicans came in and took over the product spot we was hustling out of. They just took over that spot, but we didn't know because we was in New York. So I guess they must have seen how young we was, because when they opened the door, they had a bunch of guns out. So we had to move to a different spot.

So now we on the southeast side of Washington, D.C. That area had the highest murder rate back then out of all the states. We go to the southeast side, and the street is called Elm Street. They used to call it Nightmare on Elm Street because people got shot and killed all the time. So now, I could see a bunch of them through the peephole. And we knew what they was coming for because we was hustling. So they was really coming to rob us but, remember, me and Ghost grew up robbing, so we already knew the deal. We all got the guns out.

I said, "Open the door." When they opened the door up, about six, seven dudes come in the spot and they see us with the guns out. We already out. And we like, "Yo, what you all want?" They was like, "Oh, no. What you all got?" We said, "We got walking 50s." That's what they used to call them, the pieces we were selling. They used to call them walking 50s out there. So now, we got the guns out, we sitting down. We said, "How many you all want?" They said, "No, we just want one." We knew they was coming to rob us, but once they seen how we was ready and strapped up, they walked out.

> "If these D.C. guys is on the same time that me and Ghost is on in New York, as far as robbing and trying to kill somebody for some money, they would do anything, too. And when they heard you was from New York, they didn't like New York dudes anyway."

We went to other boroughs here and there, but we really ain't messed around too much with them. Only borough that we went to go mess around with was Manhattan. And we were smoking that dust, so that was the only entrance that we had. I mean, Brooklyn was always close to Staten Island. We would steal a car. I stole a car and we would drive through there or whatever, East New York but it wasn't no . . . it wasn't our thing. We used to just turn around Staten Island. The whole Staten Island. It wasn't no limit. There wasn't no project we didn't go to and do something.

We had people, these kids from the harbor, right? And there was this guy named Leon, and he had a brother named James. So they'd be shooting their gun, too. Leon actually rode through the middle of our projects one time. And we was just sitting at a little park in front of Ghost's building, and they rode through the projects and the dude, Leon, had a gun. And he literally got out the car and chased us. And it was popping. Just barely missing my head. They wasn't afraid, neither. They was like, "All right. You all wanna do that, so this is what we gonna do."

Ghostface: Yeah. Because remember, they robbed the gun store. They had all the guns. They used to walk through the projects with knapsacks with mad guns in it. Mad guns in their shit, just a bunch of them, too. That gun store was . . . that shit was around the corner from where we lived.

Un: So it became a thing whereas, basically, we just felt like we could go anywhere. We felt like we was the toughest project, as far as fighting or whatever. Other guys in other neighborhoods knew how to fight, too. And they had guns, too. We just felt like that in our bones.

Un: Back in that time, we used to slap-box a lot. We would see who could fight the best. So we would allow a one-on-one, but if you wasn't from my neighborhood, you wasn't getting a one-on-one. We would jump you, we would do everything to you. For instance, they had the Guardian Angels come out there one time. They tried to go in every neighborhood and bring peace, calm the neighborhoods down. They made a mistake and came to our neighborhood. And even Den and Porter and them, that we didn't really like, we all got together and whipped their ass. So you probably couldn't get a one-on-one fight. Yeah, but that's how we fight. We used to watch the older dudes fight. That's how we started.

So yeah. I was getting in trouble for crimes I did and crimes I didn't do. It was just the cops would put these crimes on me, man. So for robbery. I got a rap sheet. I got everything on it. Robbery . . . only one that I didn't do was the murder. Drug shit, possession of drugs.

I never forget, right, so one day we in front of Ghost's building, right? I'd probably been home for, maybe, about three months. So when I first get out, I'm telling Ghost like, "Yo, I got to get me a job. I want to work and everything." Right? He like, "Man, fuck that job shit, man." I said, "No, I got to work. I'm not going to go back to jail." Right? So I started working on the other side of the island, the other side of Staten Island, with this white guy doing some construction.

But that working shit just wasn't for me, right? The next thing you know, I was on the bench out on the front of the building with Ghost. He gave me some cracks and I started slinging the cracks. So when I came downstairs, he said, "Yo. They got the team. That was the undercover cops. They got them up there on the roof watching us." I said, "Man, fuck them cops." I grabbed my junk, I grabbed dick where they was at, where I knew they was watching. I was like, "Yo, fuck you all." Right?

> "So when they came and bum-rushed us, right? They grabbed me and they was like, 'Yo, search him.' And he said, 'Yeah, asshole. You forgot to throw one.' I forgot to throw one crack. I had just one crack in my pocket, right? So that was just that error. That's why I was getting caught for a lot of stupid shit."

Ghostface: But then I remember the time when I went down to the precinct. Yo, because you know why? Because I told them. They caught you, they chased you down, whatever they did. They caught you in the building, I think. But I'm like, "No. My nigga can't get locked up because I love him too much." So it's like . . . I didn't want him to go for fucking four years and

Poisonous Darts

shit. So I go down [to the precinct]. I'm crazy. I went down to the precinct after I went home, I got dressed, put some knockouts on, had a little razor. Go down to the precinct and told them niggas, "Yo, listen. I did it. He didn't do it. I did it."

Un: And they still locked both of us up.

Ghostface: Like Un said, we didn't have no fear. You ain't give a fuck. It was like, "Yo. All right. Yo, my brother did it, let me go take the blame for him. Let me go take him. At least, he'd be home. I don't really got that much of a record and, hopefully, I'll come home."

Un: Yeah. I was there during the beginning of Wu-Tang. I was in videos and whatever when we really was into that. And I used to DJ. The DJ was more of my passion, which had always been around ever since we was younger. We always liked to rap. I just wanted to do it because basically Ghost was doing it, and that was the thing to do. We all was into it. So I would have been in the music with them. Because my rap name was Mickey Mirrors. They used to call me Mickey Mirrors. We used to take names out. Because we used to have all these names and I grabbed that name. We was always like that. But that's before the wrongful conviction.

That's a tough one there. So basically when we started really doing them, getting into that drug game, heavy wars, I ran into this guy around the way. We're just gonna say his name is Black, right? So I run into Black and he always been known to be with another guy called Barry Blue. Barry Blue's dead so I could say his name, whatever. So they used to get a lot of drug money when we was really young. When I came home, the guy Black is basically dick riding me, because you know he knew how wild me and Ghost was and stuff like that. And now Ghost's making the music, the Wu-Tang music is coming out, it's just starting.

So he used to hang out with him. One day he comes to me and I get inside his car, I'm in his passenger seat. He tells me he has thirty-seven birds. So I said, "thirty-seven birds, what's birds?" And he said, "kilos." I said, "Give me one." Then he got quiet and I said, "Yo, listen, we been good friends. You gonna give it to me or not." And then he told me, "Yo, all right. I got you." I go home and then I call Ghost and I'm like, yo, I said, "Yo, you know Black got kilos." And Ghost is like, "Yeah, I've been waiting for this moment. Yeah." So that's how I got that. So when we got that key and then we started making money from there.

Ghostface: We took from there, then we started elevating and then we started going to all the neighbors on Staten Island and we got the guys to basically sell the drugs for us. And the rest was history. We used to recruit other guys from other neighborhoods that was young enough, that was around our age, and now we had so much it was easier to give it to them and give them a fee out of it. So we would have a whole lot and that's how we started. And then one day RZA calls us like, "Yo, you got to stop doing that, man." He's like, "Yo, you all got to stop doing that." I never forget what he told me, man. He said you can't mix beef with pork. Meaning you can't do right and wrong and think it's gonna be all right. So we had to leave it alone.

Un: Me and Ghost were together every day. That's why I got arrested. The wrongful conviction. We was always together. We was on the road a lot. But we are into positive things now. Making the music and doing everything positive. But we always had that roughness in us. That's why the music was so like that. That's why the music was so attracting everybody because it was basically the truth. It was like, that was the way that we was living. That's why everybody was so attracted to Ghost's lyrics because what he was saying is everybody can relate, because they like, "Oh shit, I be doing the same shit." It was the truth. And somebody rhyming like that, they had to know what they was talking about.

In 1995, Redman and Method Man had a show called "The Month of the Man." The label Def Jam put them together. So we had to go to this club Palladium in Manhattan where they was doing a show. We got into a slight altercation in the parking lot because I was tired and dealing with the five hundred insane deals we was in. So me and Ghost started arguing with the guy and the guy said we robbed him, he lied on us. And next thing you know, we was in a precinct, locked up, and we didn't know what the charges was, and they put a slew of charges on us.

And then when the police see my record, they just really went crazy. They just were like, "Oh, give it to me, give me all the charges." But then we made bail and then my parole officer didn't violate me because he didn't feel like I was robbing people. He was like, "I'm not gonna bother with you." Probably because I was doing real good. So he wasn't feeling like that. That's why he never violated me. To make the long story short, I'm in there still going to court. We still got court dates together. So I still be meeting him in the pen, going to court for the shit that we had got locked up for and all that shit.

Yeah, I took the time. The same thing Ghost did for me back in 1988 I did for him later on in life. So I took the weight. I took the eight years for it, whatever. And then it ran concurrent. So we always had that brotherhood like that. And so that's how that was. He was only doing six months. Then he was able to see who he is today.

The wrongful conviction, well that happened in the beginning of '96. Things was happening in the neighborhood, and I guess people was just afraid and would throw my name up whatever situation may be. The next thing I know, they want me for a murder.

And everybody knew that I didn't do that murder. It was done in broad daylight. It was done in front of everybody, was so much crookedness with the cops with that. They had a description of the guy, the complete opposite of me. So we getting to the bottom of that right now. I was sentenced to twenty-five to life.

Ghostface: A lot of my happiness started going downhill, you know what I mean? Because it's like, for your brother, that's the closest thing to you. And then I'm dealing with diabetes shit at that time, like that. It was like, yo, I was just down and out, just down and out.

CHAPTER 3

APOLLO KIDS

Yo, check these up top murderous
Snowy in the bezel as the cloud merges
F.B.I. Try and want word with this
Kid who punked out bust a shot up in the beacon
Catch me in the corner not speaking
Crushed out heavenly, U.G. Rock the sweet daddy long fox minks
Chicken and broccoli, Wallies look stinky
With his man straight from Raleigh Durham, he recognized Kojak
I slapped him five, Masta Killa cracked his tiny form
Everybody break bread, huddle around
Guzzle that, I'm about to throw a hand in your bag
Since the face been revealed, game got real
Radio been gassing niggas, my impostors scream they ill
I'm the inventor, '86 rhyming at the center
Debut '93 LP told you to Enter
Punk faggot niggas stealing my light
Crawl up in the bed with grandma,

Beneath the La-Z-Boy where ya hid ya knife
Ghost is back, stretch Cadillacs, fruit cocktails
Hit the shells at Paul's Pastry Rack
Walk with me like Dorothy, tried to judge these
Plush degrees, sessical Rasta fiends
Getting waxed all through the drive-through
Take the stand, throw my hand all on the Bible
And tell lies too, I'm the ultimate
Splash the Wolverine Razor Sharp ring, dolomite
Student enroll holding it

[Chorus]
Aiyo, this rappin's like ziti, facin' me real TV
Crash at high-speeds, strawberry kiwi
As we approach the hood, the Gods bail
These Staten Island ferryboat cats bail
Fresh cellies, 50 deep up in the city
We banned for life, Apollo Kids live to spit the real

A pair of bright phat yellow Air Max
Hit the racks, snatch 'em up son, $20 off no tax

Street merchant tucked in the cloud, stay splurging
Rock a eagle head, 6-inch height was the bird
Monday night Dallas verse Jets, dudes slid in with one hand
Two culture ciphers, one bag of wet
Heavy rain fucked my kicks up
Wasn't looking, splashed in the puddle
Bitch laughing, first thought was beat the bitch up
Moseyed off gracefully, New York's most wanted tee-ball hawk
Seen the yellow brick road, leftover pastries
Same Ghostface, holy in the mind
Last scene, Manhattan Chase
We drew the six-eight digit in the briefcase
Rawness, title is Hell-bound
Quick to reload around faces, surround look astound

Aiyo, this rappin's like Ziti, facin' me real TV
Crash at high-speeds, strawberry kiwi
As we approach the hood, the Gods bail
These Staten Island ferryboat cats bail
Fresh cellies, 50 deep up in the city
We banned for life, Apollo Kids live to spit the real

"I started in with drugs at around fifteen. It was weed, cigarettes. You get dizzy off cigarettes, and it was probably like you smoked some weed. And then here come a bag of dust. You see the older people doing it, the guys that you look up to, that was cool around the neighborhood. You see them doing it and you want to know what they was on and shit. I mean, you know how you'd be on PCP or how you act."

I was on it, and it wasn't really that heavy. But you just did it when you did it. Like oh shit, when the man come for you, whoever got it on him. "Oh, shit, yo, let me get that. Where's it at?" Sometimes we be out there looking for it, "Yo, who got it fresh? Who got it fresh?" And stuff like that. And then you might cut it out because there was times I cut it out. Even when I went to Ohio, I cut it out. Then came back and then I dabbed back in it, maybe around '99 or something like that. And then I just cut it right off. I cut it right off. And that was it.

Because you probably out there looking stupid and shit. When you're doing that shit like that, it has an effect on you where it'll stop your movements where it's like, damn, you get stuck right there in the same spot. You be in the same spot for like two hours, and then you start to finally move because we used to get stuck in the staircases and all that shit when it's like, "Oh, shit." It's almost like *Star Trek*, because you beam back in or some other shit like that. You still got the joint in your hand. So it's like, "Oh, shit." And then you might light it back up. But some people knew how to hold it, and some people don't. I always knew how to hold it, but when a high gets you, it's like okay, you right there.

You smoke a bag away real quick, bag of dust. You're just going for the function, like how you think it is, then it's like, "Oh shit." You just going off of it and that's it, you flip the bag until you was high and then when it wears off, it just wears off and that's it. I wasn't one of them guys that'll sit there and smoke like three or four bags a day because I didn't really need all that shit, because one bag'll just drain your ass out. Yeah, really. I mean, because it was good shit back then. It was good shit.

I'm clean now, have been for many years. I drink once in the blue maybe, have a sip or something like that just to loosen you up and enjoy yourself, whatever. That happens mainly if there's a fight on TV or if I go to the club or something like that. Basically, I'm just living off life right now.

But as a teenager back in the day, I was still going through hell. While we were struggling, me and my best friend got caught. Remember I told you I deboed the video store. What happened was the next day I got bagged for that, because my friend got caught because he was picking up his brother from school. The lady was riding around in the DT car and was like, "That's him right there." They grabbed him. He gave me up. They came to my door. I got locked up for it. All right, I got a court date. Now I got to go back and forth to the courts, and they gave me about a year or so in DFY (Division for Youth correction facilities). That was upstate New York. By the time the Mets was in the World Series in '86, I had to leave around that time.

I went in for like three months, and when I came back I got my first baby mother pregnant, because you're holding all that sperm. As soon as you shoot out, you lucky if you don't get pregnant with twins. That's when my first seed got born, when I was sixteen or seventeen. He was born in '88.

I started selling my little bit of drugs and things like that. So I'm robbing and stealing and shit. I think just at that time, when you got a baby, I mean you provide, but it's like you ain't got much to get, some Pampers and some diapers and shit.

The stickup shit I pulled in my teens, maybe like eighteen, nineteen, when I did the other shit going into the stores on Staten Island, way on the other side of the island, and we would just fuck around. Run up in the store real quick, your man acting like he got the fucking gun on him. They don't got shit. He got his hand in his pocket. I have funny motherfuckers asking him why he ain't pull his gun out, because we stopped at his house and everything. "Y'all go and get the gun." Ah yeah, he came down with a hand in his pocket.

I'm the only one with a gun on me, so I don't know he ain't got the gun. We go in the store to rob the cash register and whatever else. But I'm wondering why he never pulled his gun out because he's over there at the cash register. He just taking the money, putting the money in his pocket and doing shit like that. When my other friend over here, he stealing Slim Jims and doing all this other shit. So I get in the car, ask him why he never pulled his fucking gun out. Motherfucker never had the gun on him. He was fronting. He's got his hand in his pocket.

That's the type of friends we had running around. Like, we used to trick each other. Holding out. While we in the back seat with the money, my friend is driving. "You better not be dippin' back there. You better not be dippin'." Which was exactly what we were doing. I'm sliding a hundred-dollar bill in my drawers or whatever, trying to peel off and slip it in my drawers.

I did that a few times, then went back inside. My second time they let me out, I was gone. I didn't ever go back inside. Hell, no. I was like, I ain't fucking with that shit again. I was up there and shit. Regular teenage shit. Knocked a few niggas out up there and came back, got my name up over there. Got my name up and shit and that was it. I got back to the block, that's when crack was really bubbling now. So I started working for these niggas.

Even the first time I first sold my first crack, I fucked around with it. I was selling for some other dudes at one time, but anyway, I fucked around, and I had a loaf of Wonder Bread, and I just took a couple of slices out and left 'em to get hard on the table. It took like twenty minutes for it to get hard or whatever. I crushed 'em and started filling up the capsules. Crumbs of dried-up Wonder Bread. That's how I got on. We sold it. Whacking these things. The fiends was coming back wanting their money back, but it was like, "Nigga if you don't get the fuck out my face." It's just like that. "If you don't get the fuck out, I'll punch you in your fucking face nigger, move." We whacked 'em.

> "Yeah, that's when it was going. It was different periods of my life like that where it's like, 'We'll fuck around and whack 'em.' We got like two hundred or whatever up, and we went to Park Hill and got an 8-ball. We came back and we started selling the real shit."

It was some Brooklyn cats, I think they was some Jamaicans from Park Slope. They opened up shop down where I live. But mind you before that, the Park Hill projects, they was already popping, right, because the Jamaicans was already up there. They was way better dressers than us. My projects, Stapleton projects, would just knock you out. We was more rowdy. We'd fuck you up and rob you. The projects up there, they was flossy, they was glossy. They was looking rich up there.

So I started selling for these Jamaicans down in my projects, and they was using the shit out of me because I was sitting under that building with like, thousands on me and shit. Only getting paid, I think it was about two hundred a week or something like that, or three hundred a week. Yeah, I wasn't getting paid day by day, but I was the best worker at it. Whatever I do, if I put my mind to it, I'm going to become the best fucking worker. I sat there under them buildings for hours early in the morning to like—it wasn't even no shifts. Where I'll just knock off the bombs. Yeah, I'd just knock all that shit off under the building.

I had my friends telling me, "Oh, what you doing? Oh, you're showing that stuff, oh you're gonna get in trouble." Then they fuck around and started doing this shit like that, too. Just sittin' under that building just to sell, and just getting big.

We'd post up at the front of the buildings, or we'd be on the side of the buildings moving it, or you might go in the staircase or go under the building, or go in the lobby real quick. Or you might be walking with the scene, and he hand you the money a little bit on the low, you gave him his little crash on the low, shit like that. It's like however you see it coming, it's like "Yo." You could tell him, "Just drop the money on the floor and I'm going to leave the cracks right there on the floor." It was just like that, like "Yo, just slip the money down on the floor." And then when he leave, then you might just go pick it up and as you picking it up, you drop the crack there. Yeah, you just drop the crack and go. You just got to be sneaky about it.

Slinging crack was different than any other crime I did—I mean, you could still get locked up for it, but it was just different. I'm right there under the building, all I got to do is just serve the people and get money and that's it. They had me out working like it was a job, but they didn't have me really doing shit. I just took on this shit because I needed money. So if somebody's telling you like, "I'll give you this a week. All you got to do is just do this."

Everything was an operation, but I don't know how you might look at people selling drugs and all that other shit like that. Because a lot of people that never really did it, they got different views and when you coming from the hood, it's like, "Yo, you know what? All right. Let's go up here and go buy this 8-ball real quick." Like I said, we sold the breadcrumbs before we got the real stuff.

So you chop an 8-ball and double your money or whatever the case may be, chop it up, you sell those right there and you go back up there to reup again. Small-time hustles at first, you know what I mean? You might blow your money, you might fuck around and be like, damn, I done spent a thousand dollars. I might have gambled it away in a dice game. Now you got to go and start all over again.

But then it was like, you might be sitting on ten thousand dollars and back then 10 Gs was almost like a little number to sit down on back in the '80s. And back in '86 or '87—that's not bad money for a seventeen-year-old kid. I mean, it was all right because I really never had a real "job." I did a summer youth job one year. Working for Mr. King, just raking leaves and doing all this other shit. But dude, but you were in a hot summer doing all this shit, and you only got paid every two weeks. It was like, and that shit had to go to some of my fucking school clothes. So that was probably the only real "job" I ever had in my life.

Around this time is when Un got in trouble for stealing that car and I went down to the police station to cop to the theft. Before I went down there, I armed up. I carried two razors on me, I put on some loose pants and went out to the precinct and was like, "I'm here to turn myself in. I stole the car. Grant Williams didn't do that."

The motherfuckers said, "You get in the cell, too. You're going to jail."

I wound up on Rikers Island, but that was my loyalty to my friend. I did it because I knew when he goes, he's gonna be gone for four years. I didn't really have nothing on my record at the time. I'm thinking like this, as a little person, '88 and all this type of stuff like that, I went down there and did that for my friend because I love him like that. Give me that car charge because I don't got nothing on it. Give me that shit, let him come home. I'll beat the case however I beat the case or whatever time I got to do, but I don't want my friend to go to jail.

Who does that? That's love, man. That's my loyalty. That's four years too long for you to be out of my life, bro. Yeah, we both was on Rikers Island and different houses and shit like that. Plus, he had more charges that he had to do from before, so he stayed longer, while I got out in a few months.

So when I got back out, I was back to hustling, but we would lose money. We'd try to reup a little bit of money, but it didn't always shake out. Remember we only bought the 8-ball and we tried to flip that. But we were still doing crimes and shit, sticking niggas up, and pretty soon that became a beef between Park Hill and Stapleton.

I don't know how it started, really. They was looking like they had more money than us, and we was jealous of that shit, I guess. But I know that it was animosity there, and then it became on. We would go up there because the dreads had all the weed, so we had to strap up our guns and head up there. And you had to get like twenty or thirty bags at a time, so you don't got to go back up there for a while. And we weren't buying, remember. We'd go up there, we get the weed, but we got to shoot our way out almost coming back home. They would see us coming, they be on the roofs looking at us and then they start shooting off the roof. It was like a war zone. So we'd hurry the fuck up and get back to the car as they was shooting at us, and we got back in and rode back down to our projects.

> "It was kind of scary going up there. You had to watch yourself. You don't know where that next bullet was coming from. I never shot anyone up in Park Hill that I was aware of. But shit was flying. Bullets was flying everywhere. Somebody might've got tagged."

We would do that; we ran up there and stuck up a couple of dice games. I don't know what everybody else in Stapleton was doing up there, I just know me and a few other dudes that I used to run with, we'd go up there and do that thing like that, and then make it back home.

Method Man, Raekwon and all of them, the rest of the Wu-Tang Clan, was in my project, so we just started going up there to U-God's project and robbing it. But some of the Clan members was good down in my project because they were just cool niggas and shit because we went to school with the motherfuckers. Some of us went to school with each other. But you could see a person and it's like, "Yo, just because you in my school, we go to the same school, that don't mean I know you."

We was in Junior High School 49, right in the middle of Stapleton and Park Hill. I remember Raekwon in there. RZA and them, they not from there. They're from Brooklyn, but they came later on, but they didn't go to 49. Genius is from Brooklyn, Ol' Dirty's from Brooklyn. Masta Killa's from Brooklyn, too. I think RZA's brother Divine went to 49, but RZA went to a different school when he came through. Method Man went to another school. I don't remember seeing Meth in junior high school when I was in there. It was only probably Inspectah Deck—who I didn't know at the time—Raekwon, and Cappadonna who was in 49.

I remember seeing Rae—at first me and Rae wasn't all 100 percent like that. But I remember seeing him in there because he had a lot of funny niggas he used to hang with. They had you laughing and shit, cracking jokes all day. But they was cool with the guys I grew up around. So the beef wasn't really as personal with them.

But for the most part it was like Stapleton versus Park Hill. Because we was going up there and then it's like, motherfuckers is fighting. So it became a little bit of a Stapleton part, even if the Hill wasn't thinking of it like that because they was getting more money. But to us it was the sense of it like that. And that's how a lot of shit, shooting at each other and all that happening, went down. But some of them brothers in there, they was cool.

Apollo Kids

CHAPTER 4
CAN IT ALL BE SO SIMPLE

Kickin' the fly clichés, doin' duets with Rae and A
Happens to make my day
Though I'm tired of bustin' off shots, havin' to rock knots
Runnin' up in spots and makin' shit hot
I'd rather flip shows instead of those
Hangin' on my livin' room wall, my first joint and it went gold!
I want to lamp, I want to be in the shade
Plus the spotlight, gettin' my dick rode all night
I want to have me a phat yacht
And enough land to go and plant my own sess crops
But for now it's just a big dream
'Cause I find myself in a place where I'm last seen
My thoughts must be relaxed, be able to maintain
'Cause times is changed and life is strange
The glorious days is gone and everybody's doin' bad
Yo, mad lives is up for grabs
Brothers passin' away, I gotta make wakes
Receivin' all types of calls from upstate
Yo, I can't cope with the pressure, settlin' for lesser
The God left lessons on my dresser
So I can bloom and blossom, find a new way
To continue to make more hits with Rae and A
Sunshine plays a major part in the daytime
(Peace to mankind, Ghostface carry a black 9, nigga)

Can It All Be So Simple

While I first met a lot of my Wu-Tang brothers in school, we didn't really come together until we were out on the streets. See, a lot of us dropped out of school in the tenth, eleventh grade. Hell, I never really went to high school. I started just doing other shit. When you come at a certain age, you just do what you want to do. There's no man in your life to tell you to don't do this and your mother's just the mother. So while her word I believe as family, even so, her word don't even stand some time.

Like, even when I was slingin' and dressing better, with newer clothes, new shoes everybody knew we couldn't afford, she never called me out on it. I think she might've known what I was doing, but I'm not sure because she would be busy drinking and all that. When I started smoking weed, she wanted me to do it in the house. Like, "Don't do it outside, just do it in the house." You know how mothers be. And I'm like, "Okay." I still didn't listen, though.

By this time, the situation with the younger kids was also wearing on her. That's not to say she didn't care, but like sometimes I could see it being overwhelming on a woman, it was just too much. She might want to get ahead and have her own problems, but she ain't going to bring up those problems to me, because I wouldn't understand. Maybe I would, because I was a young dude that picked up on a lot of shit, but she probably just didn't want to bring her problems to me. Sometimes you never know what somebody's going through. And she would just go to that bottle because she'd be depressed and burnt out. She could have been thinking about her two kids in wheelchairs, and my father was gone, she could have been missing my father. She could have been missing her mother, because she had passed away back then. Then you ain't straight. You got to be on welfare, and this is not what you wanted for your life, for your children's lives. I don't know what was going on in her mind, but I was doing my own thing by this time.

A lot of these motherfuckers be bragging outside like they shot someone, it's like, "But, you ain't shoot shit." And even then, even when I went over out of state, I had two more encounters like that when I got shot and I shot a dude that shot somebody else. And sticking people up there. A lot of stickups. But you know, we was young. I was in my twenties.

"One time I shot a guy over not much at all. I lent him my Gucci link. I had one girl that brought me a Gucci link when I was younger. She liked me, so she brought me a Gucci necklace, and I let somebody hold it to go to a show."

I think the dude got it snatched or whatever. He was out there like that, he came back without my chain, and I was mad. But he was talking shit and started fighting or whatever. I just got the burner. I don't know if I had the gun on me or I took it from my man and I just got on one knee and blew him, boom. And I should not have—I really shot him for nothing. I blew him for nothing—maybe because I was mad because of my chain, I just blew him and shit. I'm glad he survived, though. And I feel bad because those are one of my sins that I'm going to have to confess to the Most High, why I did that. That's one of my sins I got to take with me, I don't like really talking about my old sins and shit like that because it bothers me knowing that I'm a righteous man now. Oh, I try to be as much righteous as I can be.

"I came close to getting killed a couple of times. One was the shootout I had in Ohio. When I almost got shot in the neck. That was that time, and then in Pittsburgh I had shot the dude at the same time. And, shit, we both was in the hospital together. Side by side in the same room the next day. He's like, 'Yo, I'ma kill you, motherfucker. I'ma kill you.' He's right next to me and shit. The only thing that's blocking us is the fucking curtain. That was it."

That was in the Ohio run, right there. It's too much. And then, I'm not even going to go into all the terrorizing we was doing when we became Wu-Tang. Even one time when Biggie was performing. Biggie was performing and I bust a shot up in the Beacon Theatre, and everything just stopped. Wu-Tang was there, and I just pulled out, and I just started busting in the air. So, yeah, they shut that down.

In New York City, it was the drug hour, the crack hour. I'm going back and forth to Park Hill. It was different up there. We was looking rich. So it was just like, it was on up there. It was like a whole different town when you go up there like that.

That's when hip hop started coming. That was like when the Rakims and the LL Cool Js was playing. Even Kool G Rap was one of my favorite tapes. Slick Rick and Biz Markie. Doug E. Fresh and Lord Finesse. Those are the ones that really got me to start getting on some real rhyming shit. But before that, you had your Run-D.M.C. and your Fat Boys.

So I started rhyming in '86. Started taking it more serious, like in '87, '88. Just writing a little bit here and there. It was the glory days of hip hop for me. Special Ed and KRS-One. BDP and KRS-One dropping "The Bridge Is Over," and all this other shit. MC Shan and "The Bridge," all that shit.

Can It All Be So Simple

Then, you had a dress code that went with it, for the most part, especially up in the hill. It was nothing but Coca-Cola shirts, bamboo earrings for the chicks. But I told you, Bubbas* had silks and sharkskins. Clarks Wallabees.

And the colors . . . the Polo, Tommy Hilfiger, Nautica, back in the day those was the colors. Those was the colors, even Pacific Trail gooses. In 1988, you had Polo gooses coming through, then in the summertime you had the Polo rugbies, the Tommy Hilfiger shirts. It's like they had all different colors. And you just got like a regular pair of white shorts on or something like that with some nice sneakers. That was the shit in '88. Like being colorful, and that's where all that shit come from, and that shit stuck with us all the way to like right now.

It's just how you put your gear together. Like out the Clan, Cappadonna and Raekwon. It's like the flash nigga to me. They still rapping. They still had to put all that shit together. I see you. He come in with a pair of sneakers. I'm like, "Yo, where the fuck you get those?" You know he cool, you know how he be. He don't want to tell you where the fuck he be getting his shit from. I'm still like that. Like yo, yo, yo, you don't say nothing. Cap is like the wardrobe kingpin, like Cap will have a regular pair of pants on, but you know what? Everything else is going to be like "Oh shit yo, this nigga . . ."

Rae knows fly shit. Like fly, fly, fly, that name-brand fly shit. Like, yo, Cap had to throw colors together, but he make that shit look crazy. I'm just a mixture of what these makers is because it was them niggas I really got my shit from, fucking with Park Hill niggas back in the days, watching them. Because my projects, like I said, we just bust your ass. Take your shit. My project was take your shit. Rob you and take your shit. Them niggas was get-fly niggas. And it was like another world going up to Park Hill, looking at these motherfuckers, and the drug dealers are looking at these niggas in silk shirts and sharkskin pants with Ballys on and all that. It's like, "Yo, these niggas getting it."

It was that era, that go with all that music. And then, sometimes on the weekends, you might go to Latin Quarters. Union Square was the clubs, and Red Parrot and all that, with Bubbas wearing jewelry. Tables on. This and that, but at young ages. Young ages. So yeah. And that was, like, in the teens. That wasn't after the twenties.

One night Me, Rae, Cappadonna, Meth, RZA, Genius, Ol' Dirty, and U-God, we all battled each other before we became the Wu-Tang Clan. There was a cash prize for the winner, and the whole thing was fronted by a neighborhood drug dealer. We all did our bit and laid down our verses, but Cap fucked around and won the money, 'cause he said the drug dealer's name who had put the money up for the event. Cap spit the dude's name in his rhyme, and the crowd just went fuckin' bananas when they heard it! He stepped off with the money. But I never knew those same guys I rapped against that night would become the Wu-Tang members from Staten Island, that we'd all be in the same group one day . . . it was crazy, it was really, really crazy.

> "Yeah, at the time it was still a hobby. That was when it just started getting more clearer and clearer. So we get high, we just start spitting a few rhymes and shit like that. Niggas be smokin' woolies and shit. How do you smoke a woolie when ain't nobody rhyming? You quiet as a motherfucker."

That's when I started taking it more serious. About '89, by like '90, me and RZA had an idea, because that's when I started fucking with him. That's when we left to go to Ohio.

I first met RZA around '89–'90, through the guy I told you didn't have a gun on him when we pulled that robbery. He was a thief, and I think RZA let him hold a chain one time, and he didn't want to give the chain back and some shit like that, then they started fighting one time and shit.

When I first met RZA, like it was something about him, because he was still selling. He was a fly dude, his gear was Polo, V Goose, cables on, jewelry on, Wallabees and velour shirt and Gucci sneakers. But there was a glow over him at that time and I just felt like my soul, my spirit, just found his spirit, you know what I mean?

He was the Godbody. He was very intellectual. He had a glow about him, and I wanted to follow that glow because I knew I could learn something from him. I just knew he had something about him, that he was going to be somebody. I loved him. God just was like, "Yo, be with him." And I just followed that.

Me and RZA became mad friends. I think I knew U-God, but it was RZA, from going to Union Square and all this other stuff like that. My baby's mother lived in the Hill, she lived over there in Park Hill in the projects. So I was real close with her brother and those are her brother's friends and all that shit like that. But anybody from the Hill used to go out. They used to love to go partying in the city. There's times U-God came down and came through Stapleton, slid by my room or whatever the case may be, we just talk to kicking real quick and you keep it moving.

So some of them was cool with everybody from my town, but the rest of a lot of other people wasn't cool down there. You couldn't just walk through like that if you really know nobody.

The other reason I was getting more into writing and rhyming is that before I was messing with RZA, when I seen myself on stage, I was still doing tapes without RZA. I was still doing other stuff. And RZA was making beats and rhyming and shit at the time. RNS, aka Inspectah Deck, my man, he taught RZA how to make a couple beats and shit like that. He started RZA off, matter of fact. Deck's from the same project as me, but RZA came afterward, like a few years after we started doing this. So RZA was up in Park Hill, but I didn't really know him too-too much, like that, because they were from Brooklyn.

RZA lived in the project building next to mine, but I was at his place most of the time. We be doing that, we just got really, really close. But them brothers from the Hill like Raekwon and Method Man, they'd come down to Stapleton and record at his house.

He was in an apartment, third floor actually. We became so close that even though I lived one building over, a lot of times it was like, all right I'll crash on the couch or whatever and shit like that. It was like, yo, we over there trying to get this money any way we knew how. And he just had the music, the DJ equipment, and he knew how to make tapes. And when we weren't rapping and mixing beats, we were just chilling, drinking and smoking and watching karate movies.

In '84 and '83, the karate movies used to come on TV. On channel 5, so you know, when you was like thirteen, fourteen and all that shit like that. Brothers would come out they house doing little karate kicks and all that other shit. So you know, because you see Bruce Lee and all them motherfuckers on TV, a lot of that stuck with us. And on Forty-Second Street they had movie theaters where they showed karate movies all day. Now at thirteen and fourteen, I wasn't really going to the city. But RZA lived in Brooklyn at that time, he was going to Forty-Second Street and all that. So he got a chance to see all that movie shit that was on Forty-Second Street.

We loved karate flicks so much. Like "Oh, yo, this shit was crazy." So when we got this movie called *Shaolin and Wu Tang*, I presented him with the tape like, "Yo, you got to see this one." Because I knew he loved the karate flicks. He saw that shit and that's where he got the Wu-Tang name, like, "Yo, oh shit, we need to turn this into a group. I want to make a fucking group called Wu-Tang Clan." It took us from that day, when he said that, it took us maybe like three or four years before we put it into activation.

Mystery of Chessboxing is the karate flick I got my name from. They had fronted on him (the Ghost Faced Killer) early in the years, and the son came back like twenty years later and just started doing damage. But I fell in love with the name when I watched it, 'cause RZA had us watching all that shit, just flick after flick, but for some reason this just had a ring to it, and it was like, "Yo, that's my shit."

Can It All Be So Simple

CHAPTER 5

PROTECT YA NECK

For cryin' out loud my style is wild so book me
Not long is how long that this rhyme took me
Ejectin' styles from my lethal weapon
My pen that rocks from here to Oregon
Here's more again, catch it like a psycho flashback
I love gats, if rap was a gun, you wouldn't bust back
I come with shit that's all types of shapes and sounds
And where I lounge is my stompin' grounds
I give an order to my peeps across the water
To go and snatch up props all around the border
And get far like a shootin' star
'Cause who I are is livin' the life of Pablo Escobar
Point-blank as I kick the square biz
There it is, you're fuckin' with pros, and there it goes

Around this time I was often out in Ohio, trying to get money. That's how we bought the equipment and shit like that, and came back. We was living together, but during my time in Ohio we wasn't really talking about it. We still was talking about it, but it wasn't really like our primary thing.

When we got back, though, that's when we started really going hard. RZA got the corporation going and shit like that, and that's what it was. When I was in Ohio, he was on the Tommy Boy record label. He dropped "Ooh I Love You Rakeem," with "Deadly Venoms" (and "Sexcapades") on the EP, but it just never went nowhere. Things weren't right at Tommy Boy, but RZA still kept at it until they split in '91.

While he was doing that in New York, I was still out there on the streets. I was taking care of what I had to take care of. He's buying equipment and shit like that, making music up there on the hill. He was making music before he got to me, working with Raekwon and Meth and them, U-God and them, up on the hill. They would probably come and stay with him to lay it down. They might've laid it down at RZA's other house on Laurel, or to stay within the projects. So Method Man, Inspectah Deck, and Raekwon and U-God and them was the ones that was rhyming with Ol' Dirty, some of the Genius, he might've had some of those tracks there, but I just remember Meth, Rae, maybe Deck and U-God, who I heard on a couple of tapes.

But everybody else wasn't on there like that. Cappadonna was rhyming back then, but I never heard him on a RZA track. "I Get Down for My Crown" is one of the songs that started bringing it all together. Because when me and RZA got back together in New York, we did "After the Laughter Comes Tears" first. Then he said, "Yo, we got to go back and get the rest. Get these guys here." And these guys was nice. I said, "Yeah, you do it." Go get U-God and Meth, Rae, and put all those niggas on it. Just make the group. He got those brothers together and was like, "Yo, let's do this." And RZA knew all of them, had a personal history with everybody. RZA told them, like, "I need fifty dollars a head, just for studio time." And everybody put their money up, and there it was, and everybody would just wing it. And that's how "Protect Ya Neck" came together.

We shot the video for "Protect Ya Neck" as well, did it in black and white, very down and dirty. We had to do it ourselves, 'cause we didn't have a label. Then we made Protect Ya Neck Records after that. But I was always with RZA. That's how come when you look on the albums, I was executive producer. Me, Oli Grant, Mitchell Diggs, and RZA.

So me and RZA did the B side "After the Laughter Comes Tears." And the A side was "Protect Ya Neck."

"Protect Ya Neck" single, B side

"Protect Ya Neck" single, A side

So RZA went and got the label, pressed up records. We started bringing records to the record stores and dropping them off at colleges and doing stuff like that, doing the footwork. We put them in a record store and be like, "Yo, sell those, we give you these, we give you this, if you could sell this." All right. So we go to the college radio, we rhyming our ass off, doing all that shit, RZA still walking around trying to get a deal with a record label. If you're lucky enough to find a copy of this twelve-inch single, it goes for about fifteen hundred dollars now!

So we doing all that, and it was just like, it was every day they get on that boat, go across the water, go meet with some of these people, come back, make beats, and all that other shit. Go back out, we make records and shit, go back out there the next morning. We'd go to Manhattan, Brooklyn, dropping off records to these record stores. And the MPV, we had the MPV van, too.

MPV tour van

We just had to do the legwork, and then the radio started playing our shit. And the first one that played our shit was DJ (Kid) Capri. Shout out to DJ Capri, he was on WBLS then, his show was the first one we heard it on. He played that single "Protect Ya Neck." And I saw Rae—he was waiting for him to play it, too. He said he was going to play it. That nigga Raekwon jumped to the ceiling. I remember that shit right in the little living room, jumped right to the ceiling. "Oh shit, yo, he played our shit right now!"

Hearing something I worked on played on the radio for the first time was the best thing since having a baby. It was beautiful. It was like, you walking the block and you can hear your shit on the radio or you were in the car or something like that and shit just come on, "Wu-Tang Clan coming at you!" and it was a wreck, it was one of them grainy records. So you had that, you had Onyx on the radio, "Throw Ya Gunz," it was that era like that. Rakim's "Follow the Leader." Slick Rick's "Hey Young World." Melle Mel's "The Message." EPMD, Nas, Onyx out there at the time. You had Biggie, shit like that. And it was crazy.

When I listened to Nas back then, I was like, "Oh shit! He fucking murdered that." That forced me to up my own writing game, like, "How can I do it like this nigga's doin' it?" The whole *Illmatic* album forced me to take my shit to another level. It was a true inspiration.

And from right there, we started taking off. Shit started getting hot. Now you got labels that's coming at you now. And niggas was looking for the record and the record stores. That's why we began to perform.

RZA went to all the labels. And then he went to see Def Jam and Russell Simmons, and Russell, he wanted to take the whole group. But RZA said, "No, I don't," because he had a plan like, "Yo, I'm going to bring the group up. But I want to get a deal where everybody could go single-handedly and get they own shit." It wasn't one deal that could just lock everybody in as a group. We wanted everybody to go solo. Like, all right, we do this, but we got the option to go somewhere, so that main label, if they can't match what another label's doing, they got to let us go. If they want to match it and keep us, all right, cool.

Russell turned us down because he didn't want to give us that deal, he wanted everybody. He said nobody's going to do it like that. So we went to Steve Rifkind from Loud Records. RZA met with him and he offers us a deal, like, "You know what, I don't got no money, but what I could do, I could get you out there. I can get you everywhere you got to go. I can get you this and get you that." And he said "I can promote you very, very well. I can get you there, and I give you the deal that you want to go anywhere you want to go to. But please let me have first dibs on it. Like the first option to see if I can match that. If I can't match it then you can just go.

But let me just, let me see if I can match it first." He was offering a small advance. Probably got like thirty Gs to do the album. That was just mixing and listening.

Inspectah Deck, Ghostface, and Steve Rifkind

Meanwhile, RZA had mad offers he went to, but I don't really remember because he was the one that was riding the shit. He was the captain, so he was doing all that shit. They'd go up to the meetings or whatever they did. Sometimes we might be in the office, sometimes we might not. So sometimes he went by himself.

I think RZA just trusted his gut feeling and Rifkind said the right shit. Before RZA made the deal, I don't know if he talked to everybody about it, I think he might've came back—I'm not sure, I think he did probably come in and say something like, "Yo, well, these guys offering this and this one's offering that and this and that and the third. But I think we should go with this."

RZA's a genius. That's why I walked with him every step of the way. Because he knew the ins and outs. He the one that changed that law like, "Nah man, you ain't get to keep everybody. We going to go do our separate ways." Shit like that. You can't hold everybody like that. Nah.

"We don't want you to just sign as a group, no, we want to be able to go in each way." And they said, to RZA, I think he said they said that, "Oh, nobody's going to do that. Nobody's going to do that." You know what I mean? And then we ran into Steve Rifkind.

> "That's why Rifkind got Raekwon for *Cuban Linx*. By that time I was the next one, and I was going to Sony. That's why Dirty went over to Elektra. That's why Genius went over to Geffen. And Def Jam, they offered Method Man more money, I guess, so they had him and shit like that. That's why Meth ain't on there. Like, everybody was already going with they own little side projects and shit."

But even with all that going on, we had to lay down a record for Loud. We already had shit in the bag anyway. We had recorded "C.R.E.A.M." I think we did "Can It Be All So Simple" in the house, if I'm not mistaken. I think "Bring Da Ruckus" was in the house. Even "Method Man" was recorded in the house.

And that's why RZA had enough to bring to those labels right there, like that. To show them like, "Yo, this what we got here. Listen, man, this shit is the real deal." He didn't just go with "Protect Ya Neck," he brought the tracks that were recorded in his apartment. On his little four-track machine.

WU-TANG

1991
Words From The Genius
(The Genius)

1993
Enter The Wu-Tang (36 Chambers)
(Wu-Tang Clan)

1994
Tical
(Method Man)

1995
Return To The 36 Chambers: The Dirty Version
(Ol' Dirty Bastard)

Only Built 4 Cuban Linx...
(Raekwon)

Liquid Swords
(Genius/GZA)

1996
Ironman
(Ghostface Killah)

1997
Wu-Tang Forever
(Wu-Tang Clan)

1998
The Pillage
(Cappadonna)

The Swarm
(Wu-Tang Killer Bees)

RZA As Bobby Digital In Stereo
(RZA)

Tical 2000: Judgement Day
(Method Man)

1999
Wu-Chronicles
(Various Artists)

Beneath the Surface
(Genius/GZA)

The RZA Hits
(various artists)

Nigga Please
(Ol' Dirty Bastard)

Blackout
(Method Man and Redman)

Uncontrolled Substance
(Inspectah Deck)

Golden Arms Redemption
(U-God)

Immobilarity
(Raekwon)

PROJECTS

2000
Supreme Clientele (Ghostface Killah)

Ghost Dog: Way of the Samurai (Soundtrack) (RZA)

The W (Wu-Tang Clan)

The Yin and the Yang (Cappadonna)

2001
Wu-Chronicles: Chapter II (Various Artists)

Digital Bullet (RZA As Bobby Digital)

Bulletproof Wallets (Ghostface Killah)

Iron Flag (Wu-Tang Clan)

2002
The Trials and Tribulations of Russell Jones (Ol' Dirty Bastard)

Legend of the Liquid Sword (GZA/Genius)

2003
The World According to RZA (RZA)

The Struggle (Cappadonna)

The Movement (Inspectah Deck)

Birth of a Prince (RZA)

The Lex Diamond Story (Raekwon)

2004
The Pretty Toney Album (Ghostface Killah)

Tical 0: The Prequel (Method Man)

No Said Date (Masta Killa)

Disciples of the 36 Chambers: Chapter 1 (Various Artists)

718 (Ghostface Killah and Theodore Unit)

2005
Osirus: The Official Mixtape (Ol' Dirty Bastard)

Mr. Xcitement (U-God)

A Son Unique (Ol' Dirty Bastard)

Put It on the Line (Ghostface Killah and Trife Da God)

2006
Fishscale (Ghostface Killah)

The Resident Patient (Inspectah Deck)

Made In Brooklyn (Masta Killa)

4:21 The Day After (Method Man)

More Fish (Ghostface Killah)

2007
The Big Doe Rehab (Ghostface Killah)

8 Diagrams (Wu-Tang Clan)

2008
Digi Snacks
(RZA As Bobby Digital)

The Cappatilize Project
(Cappadonna)

Pro Tools
(GZA)

GhostDeini the Great
(GhostFace Killah)

2010
Manifesto
(Inspectah Deck)

Wu-Massacre
(Method Man/ Ghostface Killah/ Raekwon)

Apollo Kids
(Ghostface Killah)

2012
Wu-Block
(Ghostface Killah)

Selling My Soul
(Masta Killa)

2014
Hook Off
(Cappadonna)

A Better Tomorrow
(Wu-Tang Clan)

36 Seasons
(Ghostface Killah)

2009
Slang Prostitution
(Cappadonna)

Blackout! 2
(Method Man/ Redman)

Dopium
(U-God)

Wu-Tang Chamber Music
(Various Artists)

Only Built 4 Cuban Linx... Pt. II
(Raekwon)

Ghostdini: Wizard of Poetry in Emerald City
(Ghostface Killah)

Afro Samurai (Soundtrack)
(RZA)

2011
Shaolin Vs. Wu-Tang
(Raekwon)

The Pilgrimage
(Cappadonna)

2013
Twelve Reasons to Die
(Ghostface Killah)

Czarface
(Inspectah Deck)

Eyrth, Wynd and Fyre
(Cappadonna)

The Keynote Speaker
(U-God)

2015
Sour Soul
(Ghostface Killah and BadBadNotGood)

Fly International Luxurious Art
(Raekwon)

Every Hero Needs a Villain
(Inspectah Deck)

Twelve Reasons to Die II
(Ghostface Killah)

The Meth Lab
(Method Man)

The Pillage 2
(Cappadonna)

Once Upon a Time in Shaolin
(Wu-Tang Clan)

2016
Anything But Words
(RZA)

A Fistful of Peril
(Inspectah Deck)

2018
Venom
(U-God)

Czarface Meets Metal Face
(Inspectah Deck)

Ear Candy
(Cappadonna)

The Lost Tapes
(Ghostface Killah)

Meth Lab Season 2: The Lithium
(Method Man)

2020
The Appetition
(Raekwon)

Black is Beautiful
(Cappadonna)

S.M.T.M. (Show Me The Money)
(Cappadonna)

2022
Saturday Afternoon Kung Fu Theater
(RZA)

Slow Motion
(Cappadonna)

Czarmageddon!
(Inspectah Deck)

Meth Lab Season 3: The Rehab
(Method Man)

RZA Presents: Bobby Digital and The Pit of Snakes
(RZA)

Da Illage
(Cappadonna)

3rd Chamber Grail Bars
(Cappadonna and Stu Bangas)

Digital Potions
(RZA as Bobby Digital)

2017
The Wild
(Raekwon)

Loyalty is Royalty
(Masta Killa)

The Saga Continues
(Wu-Tang Clan)

2019
Czarface Meets Ghostface
(Ghostface Killah and Inspectah Deck)

Thriller (Soundtrack)
(RZA)

Chamber No. 9
(Inspectah Deck)

Ghostface Killahs
(Ghostface Killah)

The Odd Czar Against Us
(Inspectah Deck)

2021
Black Tarrzann
(Cappadonna)

Super What?
(Inspectah Deck)

2023
African Killa Beez
(Cappadonna)

36 Chambers wasn't sonically like crystal clear, but I think people gravitated to it because it was on tape. It didn't sound like no CD. It sounded like a fucking tape. You could still hear the fuck-ups on it. You could hear the wall, it was warm. You can still hear the fuzziness in it.

So, yeah, so it's just crazy on how it came. It had to come. The Clan had to come, me and my brothers. *The 36th Chamber of Shaolin*, yo, that's a karate movie. Thirty-six chambers. So it took them thirty-six chambers to reach to the top. And then when you add three and six together, that makes nine. Right? So there was always like nine members, plus the DJ, inside the crew. And it was crazy. It was just so put together that I wouldn't ever change nothing. Even if I could have got the sound crystal, I wouldn't change it because for some reason I think it was so raw. People gravitated to that.

> "It sounded dope as fuck. Hearing it like that all put together because we left RZA alone in there and let him put the karate skits where they needed to be. Let him do the track order. That's what people don't know about albums. You got to really put your songs in order to see which sound good coming after another. Just to keep the person's attention right there."

And then we added karate flicks. We added a sense of humor to it. Character, we added character to it. As far as the skits. And then you got scientists that's just rhyming on it? Like Genius, RZA? Method Man come with all these fucking styles. Then you got me and Rae, Inspectah Deck. Like it was too many dangerous MCs at that time on that one project right there. And it's always been a mystery. It was a mystery, like everybody wasn't on the album cover. You might see like seven people on the album cover, but some of those people is other people. Method Man got locked up smoking weed during the album-cover shoot, so he wasn't there. Masta Killa wasn't there either. But we all had masks on, so you don't know who was who.

And then it became almost like a cult. Wu-Tang became like a cult, like, "Oh shit, you got so many people." It was like Earth, Wind & Fire of rap. Like, "Oh shit, he's got all these motherfuckers in there. Who's who? Who's that? Who's that? Who's that? Who's that?" You know what I mean? And shit like that. So, yeah, it was crazy.

Now I'm starting to make records, but I'm still trying to get my dab and other shit. Probably did that shit for a couple of years, dealing with kilos or shit like that. It was just like, you might get your little big eights and all that other shit and, you know, make your money off shit, but like I said, like ten, fifteen grand or whatever it was. It wasn't like I was moving millions, and I was getting caught doing all that. I wasn't a New York Scarface or anything.

But it was just like, yo, I'm getting rap money now, and I had to make a decision. I remember one day RZA said, "Yo, what you gonna do, bruh? You can't mix pork with beef, man. You gotta do one or the other.'" I had to make a decision, and that was it.

So I just stopped it. I got out of the game.

At the time, we were doing a lot of college runs, college radio at first, and all that. Yeah, we'd just go, like, whatever they had for us to do. You got to do promo. So we wasn't getting paid for a lot of these gigs. Anywhere they'd send us, we was there. We'd just get in the van and go, that's all. Because the record was hot. It started blowing up. We was all new, aiming for the same shit. We ain't have that many solo artists. Everybody was just in one shit, so you can't say, "Yo, this is my shit." Or, "I got something to do over here." No, we all did it all together, and that was it.

Protect Ya Neck

Being in the van with the Clan was like a brotherly thing, because now you live in this. You live in this, and you live in it among your brothers. You were enjoying being among your brothers. And you know, you ain't got nothing else better to do. You seeing the world. You seeing another place you never went to, right. It's like your record is popping. You're doing all that, you're trying to work your record. You flying, you DJing, you know me, you out, you're away from home.

You here with them like that. It was no, "Oh, Ghostface got to do this." Or, "Ghostface got his own single over here." Or, "Method Man got a job over here. He got to do that." Or, "Rae got to go over there." We was all there to make it work, and when you feel yourself blowing up, you want to come to work. "Oh, shit. Oh, word? This is what we was doing?" Because it just went up. It was like, before you know it, we're doing a fucking arena. We're doing arenas and shit after a while, and you getting bitches. Talking to these bitches on the road, and doing all this other shit. It was like, a young dream. And you in your early twenties. In your early twenties. I seen it. I told you I seen it in my mind first, but the reality was like, "Wow." From the time I seen it, and then really get that, remember I told you, it took, like, five years from the time I seen it. I think I first seen it in '87—'87 to '93, like, five to six years. But in the mix of all that, I got shot for this shit. I had to bang a few, too. And just all that. So I get what praise is due, because I came up out of that.

Of course, the road wasn't always good to us either. I remember one time we went to Houston, Texas, and they chased us out the building. I was in Fifth Ward at this club, they had a Scarface mural on the wall, and I don't even think we was getting paid for this shit, but I just felt divided. So when I went in there, I said, "Yo, man, I don't feel right in here." I said, "Everybody, just be careful, just be careful. Yo, stick together."

And one of the guys, he's performing, and one of the guys in the crowd said something, and RZA asked one of them, you know, "What the fuck? What'd you say?" So when he gave him the mic, he said, "What'd you say?" RZA couldn't understand. RZA gave him the mic and he said,

"Yo, get that fucking shit out of here. We don't want to hear that shit." And before you know it, the kid threw something at RZA, and RZA just threw a fucking Heineken bottle at this motherfucker, and it was all from right there, and we had to run out the back doors. Trying to find a way to the van, get in, and just keep going. They was hitting in the van with bricks, every fucking thing, and they could carry guns, too. And in Texas, it was like, it was his army. They chased us out of there, though. Yep, and they gave us a fucking fake hundred-dollar bill. You got paid a hundred dollars, and it's a phony.

On that day, Ol' Dirty saved the day because we didn't know how to get the fuck out there. He just said, "Go down that way, make the right, go down that way, you just go down that way," and we just drove . . . the guy that was driving just drove, and there it was, there was a little opening inside the gate, and we made out, because if you didn't go out that time, we would have been full of these motherfuckers.

About this time is when we got booked on *The Arsenio Hall Show*. It was big. Now remember, we were still young. It was still fresh to us. Really, you know, we just did what we had to do. And that was it.

It wasn't so much pressure. It's like when you on that stage, and you're just going in front of the audience, you do feel like a little nervous, a little nervous and shit like that. I wasn't scared. We wasn't scared. It wasn't like I was going by myself anyway. I would have been more scared if I was by myself probably, but, yo, you know, the magnitude is on, and then you get these, these cameras, and all that shit is there like now. But I'm with my brothers. I got, I got nine other brothers with me, so it was like, I just got to do my part, and hopefully it will be over.

I don't even know if it did move the needle. It's just like we just did it, and you gone, you ain't around really nobody. Cell phones wasn't really popping like that. It's like you don't get no feedback, so you just do it and kept it moving. All right. cool, we just did that, we smashed that.

When we started blowing up, it was just, I don't even remember, crowds just was coming. I'm twenty-three, twenty-four years old, I'm not paying attention. Word, I'm just in the mix, I'm in the mix. Oh shit, oh word, you just go with the flow. I didn't pay attention to none of that shit. I'm just like we getting money, we on screens, I know what's going on. I know what type of crowd we got. I don't know if the TV show lifted up like that.

With our solo projects, we planned it according to who was hottest at the time, because it made the most sense. It was like, if Meth is the hottest nigga, you put him out first. It was like, "Yo, Meth, who's the next hot nigga?" If Ol' Dirty's the next hot nigga, put Dirty out. "Okay, yo, here go Rae right here." And Rae was the next one. And then at the same time with Rae, here come Genius. And then came me. And that's how it went. Whoever's popping the most, they go down the line. "All right, yo Meth, you first. All right, yo, we're going to do Dirt. Dirt, yeah, yeah, all right Dirt. All right, yo, Dirt. All right, Dirt doing his shit. All right, yo, Rae." Then go Rae. Rae's coming after Dirt, you know what I mean?

With *Cuban Linx*, me and Rae had the chemistry, like we was both street dudes. I was out there more, and before we had the Clan, Rae was out there getting money with him and his homies. And I'd be down in my project getting money, me and my mans and shit. And I'm one of them niggas that'll rob you. I would be out there robbing and doing all types of shit, you know what I mean? So our shit just went together.

But Rae was always a slick dude on the mic. He'd talk a lot of slick shit. And it's like, being around him and shit, he opened up a new lane for me. Like street raps and metaphors. So I got that from Rae. Like more street. I like to make movies when I write. I like to paint pictures, tell ill stories and shit. That's my lane more than just a regular rap.

So when I got with Rae, I still did my stories, but he opened me up to more than just saying a bunch of flash shit and putting words together like that. He's what opened me up more to that shit right there. And remember, we're still in our prime. We still like twenty-three, twenty-four, twenty-five. We going in, you know what I mean? Still stealing shit. Like I told you, I had the best of both worlds, because I got this, my rhyme's going off. I'm down in my projects, still cutting up, breaking down kilos and shit. And it was like you right there, your mind is open, doing everything, you know what I mean?

That meant the way me and Rae came together, it just went perfect. So even when you got the skits off the *Cuban Linx* album, me and Rae together, just me and Rae, we riding around. We got the microphone on and I'm just telling these niggas like, "Yo, we're going to kill them this year." Because we was just trying to find some skits that we could do to bring back to the studio to put on his shit. So we had the DAT, a little digital audiotape machine, with the skits on it and shit. Little microphone, it was portable. And we just recording, come out crystal clear. And that's how you got the skits on Raekwon's album. All the "blue and cream" shit and all of the other shit, whatever skits we did, that all came from riding around.

I remember I said, "Yo, it feel hot at night." It was one day in the summer and it felt mega hot, you know? At night, though, at night. And that's the shit that we fucked around and put before . . . I think that skit was before, "Line for line, is how we get down" on "Spot Rusherz." "Line for line, line for line, this is how we get down." That was that skit that went before that track.

While we were recording, we wanted to get out of the city. We wanted to get away and go write the album, which was a good idea. So I'm up there looking at pamphlets and shit, and I see some shit in the Barbados called the Royal Pavilion, and it just looked alive on the brochure.

So Rae agreed to go, like, "Let's try this, let's go to Barbados, kid." Because you think of Barbados, you think about sunshine. And the way the shit sound, the shit just sound fly. We got there, but the shit was never like the fucking pamphlet. Yo, because that's how they get tricky, they trick you. That's with anything. They glossed the menu up, and then when you get your fucking burger bag, it don't even be the same shit. It's like a commercial.

So I get there, we get there, and it's all good, or whatever the case may be. I think we have fatigues on when we was coming through there, and even the Black people was looking at us like, "Yo." Like we ain't belong there, since we got there. We got the music on, they come banging on the door. "Oh, yo, you got to turn it down..." But the music ain't even blasting like that. We got our own shit, you know what I mean?

We trying to write, do all this other shit, and they keep coming. Every fucking day (at the hotel) is a problem with these fucking people. They might've still been some type of... where the white man still got them in check, you know what I mean? Like a slavery thing. But they still on some other shit in that hotel at that time. I don't even know if they was really popping at that time, the way they was acting, you know what I mean?

So we'd just tell them like, "Yo, we ain't bothering nobody." Because they kept sending security to the room. And it just got too much. And then one day they said, "Oh, you can't wear that here. You can't wear that." And we're like, "Yo, what the fuck? It's fatigues." When they came up with that shit, we got the fuck out of there. We just got the fuck out. We made a phone call. "All right, fuck it, let's go to Miami. Let's just go to Miami then."

And that was the best thing we did. Because we were Scarfaced out over there. It was like, yo, shit felt like Scarface just left. Crazy vibe. Yeah. The vibe was crazy. The music is coming. I'm like, "Yeah, this the shit." And we had all those beats on us right there, too. Man, we just went right in. We were just going in every night, just writing fly shit, sitting there, putting the music on, Rae's smoking, lighting his shit up. I might have a little six-pack of Heineken right here. And we just darting every day. "Check out the rap kingpin, the Black Jesus. / I know a few niggas sniff coke, it cause seizures." The lines just kept coming.

Everything was just coming together. And then we'd go outside, we bump into Tony Touch. That's when we first met Tony Touch. He was a DJ in Miami. So we got real close and shit. So he fucking with us. We were just out there. And we just knocked all the verses out, came back to the city, and laid it down, for the most part. We still had more versions to do. Because Rae recorded "Incarcerated Scarfaces" at the studio on Staten Island in, I think, in RZA's crib. No, I think it might've been in Jersey. Yeah. So we just went and knocked that out and came back with the goal.

We was there through the whole shit. The order. Even with taking the shit from *Scarface*, when we did "Criminology." When you get the *Scarface skit*. What did he say? "You fucking monkey. You want a war? You want a war?" Put that in there like that, boom. "Yo, take that and put that at the top of 'Criminology,' right up in there like that." Even *The Mack*. *The Mack* came in like, "Yo." You know what I mean? With "No dough." That was before "Wisdom Body." It just flowed so good because we in there, we was on our mafioso shit. That's the times when the mafia was still lit, you know what I mean? John Gotti and all these other guys. We in there, got all that. That's how the names came up, like Wu-Gambino and Maximillian, GZA was Maximillian, and all this other shit like that. We had all these names, Johnny Blaze and Rollie Fingers and Lucky Hands and Bobby Steels and all the other shit like that. That's when a lot of rappers started using a lot of those names like that. Masta Killa was called Noodles, after the dude from *Once Upon a Time in America*. Another flick with Robert De Niro and all that shit. Rae put me onto that movie. That's where the whole Wu-Gambino thing came from—mafia movies and Rae and me.

CHAPTER 6

RAINY DAYZ

On rainy days I sit back and count ways on
How to get rich, son, show and prove, ask my bitch
Stood up late nights, build with my a-alikes
We can pull a heist, snatch ice or rock mics
But this rap shit, got me wanna clack back the latch
How it goes the only pesos made from scratch
But in due time, soon to get mine like Bugsy
Heavy on the wrist, Polo mocs, socks and rugbies
Old flicks remind me of Gucci's
Back in Union Square when little Maxmil blast Pierre
That was Build Build, fast forward, ninety-four
Who got the bad base? Filthiest fiends scream for more
Bless me out of state, howdy Jake, Starks is back
Niggas want work, nine brought back off a g-pack
Coke rocks flood the co-ops, live in gossip
Them big lip niggas singing to cops need to box it
Stop it, the projects over-flooded with slow leaks
The fiends geek, new faces get wrapped in sheets
I gotta get mine, like my old Earth, bless the cheese line
Sipping on fine wines, the power of the blacks refined

(Rainy days) Divine
Waiting on these royalties takes too long
It's like waiting on babies, it makes me want to slay thee
But that's ungodly, so, yo, God, pardon me
I need it real quick, the dough flow like penmanship
Meatheads get pistol-whipped, I blow spots like horse shit
So now talk shit, nigga, what?

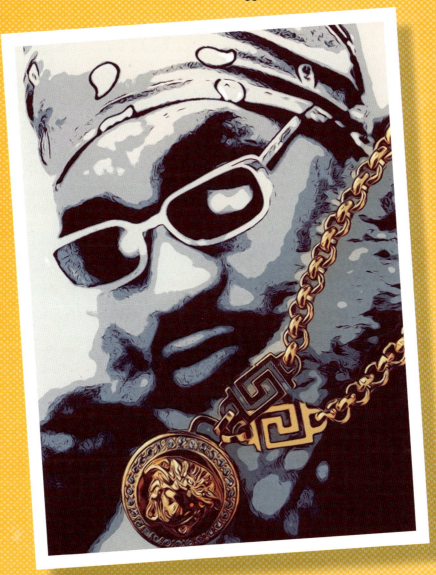

While we were putting down the tracks for *Cuban Linx*, certain aspects of my mental state were coming to a head, so to speak. To this day, it's still something I have to deal with. None of that is ever going away, so I just have to live with it and deal with it the best I can.

When I was in Ohio and I got shot and shit, I was smoking some weed, and I went to go lay down and try to take the high off. That's when I heard voices like something came across my head. Felt like a pool of water just splashing the side of my head while I was laying down. I don't even know if it was water. It was something that felt like it just dripped inside my head. I'm in the room, alone. I don't know if it was a panic attack or something like that. Like I couldn't even hold a cup of water. So I got up and just started doing some pushups like, "Oh, please, please go along, please, please get this off me." I kept hearing voices, "I got you. I got you. I got you. I got you now. I got you now." But it was whispering. It was always just whispering.

So at first I just tried to ignore it. But when I woke up the next day, I didn't feel right. I didn't feel like myself. Like I just felt like I saw fuzziness everywhere I looked. Like back in the day when you got the channel 1, channel 3—it was like all fuzziness. Like that's how my sight and everything was. And even when I looked in the mirror, my face looked kind of strange. And even I could remember my brother was telling me, like, "Yo, what's wrong with your face?" And I'm just trying to, like, not paying it no mind.

It was visible to other people, but sometimes people don't say nothing. But he had witnessed it in the morning. And it just had me stuck there, like looking in the mirror trying to be like, "Yo, I'm trying to figure it out." And my left side, it felt a little bit off. It felt off. I really can't get it. Like, I don't know. It just felt, it's a feeling that you can't even all explain. But remember I got shot in the left side of my neck, too.

"So I don't know what was the cause . . . you know what I mean? Like was it the weed? Or the gunshot? That like both of them together? I'm not sure. But anyway, whatever it was, it just led to days and days of this shit, like I had to ignore it all the way to this day."

But I took all that same energy with me, you know, when I got back home. I started like really like thinking, 'cause a lot of weird shit started happening. I get this piece of paper one day in the mail and it's showing like, you know, like a couple of symptoms I had, as far as depression. That if you have depression, you feel like this. Panic attacks or shortness of breath, heart palpitations. And there's a couple of those things that I had that was on the paper. But you know, I talked to myself, I really never told nobody and shit, so yeah.

So then when I get back home, it's still on, but I'm, you know, I'm drinking, and when I drink, it just takes a lot of shit off. So when I was doing, like, all those tracks on Raekwon's album, that's when I think I might've seen the doctor. I seen what the fuck this was like, yo. Hold on, I need a psychiatrist? Some motherfucker just telling me to do shit. Just telling me to do this and that and the third. Shit was like where you couldn't control your thoughts. It made me a lot more quiet. It made me more quiet cause I didn't really want to talk too much. So I mainly lived in my mind for the most part. And then when I'm drunk, okay, it'll take the edge off and loosen me up.

This is how my life has shaped. It's like I'm well aware of a lot of things. I've been to psychiatrists and all that shit from the diabetes making me feel like I was bugging out and all that. Not knowing I was a diabetic. Eating all these pills in '95 and seeing shit and hearing voices. I had to beat that mental devil right there that was trying pull me away from real life. People don't understand, don't know this shit. That's why mental illness is a real thing. I used to tell my best friend, "Yo, I'm bugging right now. Something is speaking to me. Telling me to jump in front of this train or to jump off the roof." I'm doing a photo shoot and it will tell me to jump off the fucking roof.

We would do photo shoots. Yeah. The photographer would tell you like, "Yo, just do that, do that, do this. Like, don't jump off this shit." And I wouldn't get no closer. I don't like heights. I don't like sitting on the edge next to nothing. But this shit was making it seem like you could have did it. And just . . . and that was it. But it's like, something was like, "Just don't even stand over there." 'Cause I couldn't take the chance.

It's talking to me like that. I used to tell RZA, "Something is telling me to punch you in the face. It's telling me right now." RZA is so smart, he would break down the brain on me. He would talk to me and tell me what part of the brain is this and this. Whatever it was, whether I smoked some weed that day and it had me thinking crazy or whatever the case, it's like I'll be back to normal because he sat there for an hour and took me through it. Every time he would break it down on me, he made that feel better. Riz is like a scientist, a doctor, so he talks to you about the mind and the brain and all that. It'll have me feeling way better because I can tell him. I can walk to him, I'll tell him I'm going through it. Shit'd tell me to punch anybody in the face. I told him like, "Yo, shit's telling me to hit you right now." And that's how I know some people might be killing motherfuckers, because they might be going through that and don't even know. And they just follow what they mind is telling them to do.

All it was, was just therapy for me. I needed his therapy. My friends would be like, "Yo, you don't need that medicine. You ain't crazy." But when I drank, it took everything away, but when I wasn't drinking, it would be back on me. All these questions and shit like that. It was bothering me physically, you know what I mean? It would cause me to really be in a shell and be quiet, because I had so much stuff. Almost like I couldn't control it. After I seen a psychiatrist and they was giving me all those pills, my man is telling me, "You ain't bugging out." When I'm drunk I'm going to be like, "What the fuck is wrong with me because I don't feel this shit?"

Now I've trained myself to ignore it. The more I ignored it, the more I got away from it. It tried to come back years later, but I'm like, ignore it. Just don't even think about it. Ignore it. People don't really know. I was writing "Fire" in '95 because me and Raekwon did the *Cuban Linx* album. My friends would say, "You're writing all this fucking murder. What the fuck is wrong with you? You're not crazy." I couldn't understand how I was writing that shit. You see what I'm saying? It was just like, "Damn, how the fuck I move my arm? How am I looking out through my eyes? How am I hearing my own voice as I'm talking to you? How am I hearing my own voice?" Questions that normal people don't ask themselves. If you just know your arm goes up, but you don't even know that your brain is controlling it because you forget about your brain controlling your arm, you're just doing it, but me, it was in me. Damn, what made my skin black? I'm feeling my face, how do I feel? How do I feel my hand on my face? Where does the feeling come from? You start asking yourself all of this and bugging yourself out.

And people don't know that's in my mind at that time. Doing all this music. I don't know how it came in, or not, but it wasn't good for me. It wasn't good. It's like what if I would have just jumped in front of the train? Or jumped off that roof? I didn't want to go on roofs. I didn't want to do that for photo shoots and stand up there and do that and I didn't like that. I kept hearing . . . You could tell me "bye" at the end of a sentence, "All right, bye." And I'll just keep hearing, "Bye. Bye. Bye. All right, bye. All right, bye." Just keep hearing it like an echo in my mind and my ears. Imagine that. That's why I say the Most High God, he kept me hidden. He just kept me here like that with a little bit of strength to fight this demon that was all over me.

> "So that's what I had. That's what happened with me. But, you know, I was keeping it to myself. RZA knew a couple of things because I tell him, like, 'Yo, this shit right here is—there's something that's telling me to do this and do that.' And RZA is sitting next to me, and he'll fuck around and break down the brain on me, telling me like, 'Yo, this and that and that.' He made me feel better."

I was just a little bit stronger to not jump off a roof or go punch this motherfucker in his face or shoot this motherfucker. That's why I said I'd rather just not say nothing to nobody. A lot of times it just . . . I like for the most part to just keep it cool. When I got something to drink, then I start questioning myself. What the fuck is wrong with me? I know I'm not bugging. I had that fight, and that's what led me to seeing these . . . seeing a couple of doctors like psychiatrists or shit like that. They start trying to toss you medicine.

Like one day I woke up my father, and he brought me to, you know, one of these people in Jersey and they started showing me like little square pictures of . . . you know how they put the paint on the card? What this look like to you? Like butterflies or like little paint, little splash of paint on it. And I'm like, I'm getting mad at them. 'Cause it's like, I'm not, I ain't no stupid motherfucker. It's like, what the fuck is y'all showing me this shit for? Like it looks like nothing. It just looked like a picture of white cardboard with some paint splashed on it.

So a doctor's giving me all types of shit. Gives me all types of shit. Klonopin, Luvox, and some other shit. But all that shit did was, like, break me out. Like I felt like little bumps coming on my hands and shit. And they're like, "Nah, this ain't the one, yo, this ain't the one." And I'm telling my psychiatrist like, "Yo, I feel mad. Like weak and sluggish." He took me to his doctor across the street. That's how I found out I was diabetic. They took my sugar and it was 500. So he came back like, "Yo, your shit is off the records. 500. You're a diabetic." I said, "Oh, shit." So I'm still dealing with the other problem.

But the only reason I beat that shit or suppressed it is that I was writing. So when I go back to the crib where we was all staying at in Jersey, doing the *Cuban Linx* album, I was writing "Murder Spree."

Anyway, we slid to Miami after that and finished the album. But in the mix of that, I'm recording shit in the house when we get back and laying all these verses down. And I'm telling one of my brothers in the kitchen something like, "Yo, I'm bugging, y'all. I'm on it like this. I got this medication." 'Cause I really didn't tell all the people. And he's like, "Yo, man, you ain't bugging. You ain't bothering no one, bro. You ain't bugging." So I just picked up the shit to be like, "Yo, you know what, man? Whatever it's telling me do, ignore it. Ignore it, ignore it, ignore it." And that's how I got through it. By ignoring it.

> "But that's not to say the problem is not still there. 'Cause sometimes the devil could come back in and try to fuck with you. I'd rather have my bones broken in my body than deal with a mental or mental fucking . . . something's telling you to do shit like that, because it's almost like you can't control it. It's like you can't control it because it's in your fucking head. It's just there. You wake up, it's there."

So I ignored it the best way I could. And then the more I ignored it, the more, the further away it went. The further away it went. It's almost like you're not giving it a place to live. It's just there until I fuck around and drink or get drunk, then it just go away. Until this shit just came off my back. So that this lasted for like a few years. Maybe three years or some something like that. You're going through shit. Three or four years, during which we're rushing around and doing all of this shit, writing, performing, all this stuff, running around the country.

CHAPTER 7
RISE OF THE IRONMAN

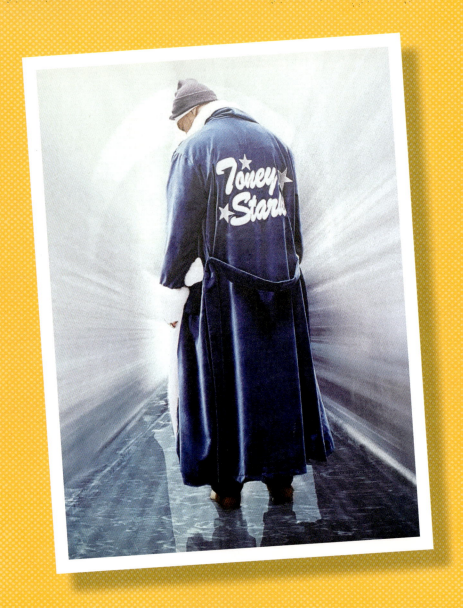

RISE OF A KILLAH: Ghostface Killah

We eat fish, toss salads, and make rap ballads
The biochemical slanglord'll throw the Arabs
In the dope fiend, vocal chords switch laser beams
My triple sevens broke the slot machines out in Queens
Grey Poupon is Revlon rap, smack pawns, swing like batons
Most my niggas smoke like Hillshire Farms
Check the gummy sole, underneath my shoe lies the tap
That attract bow-legged bitches with wide horse gaps
In steel mills Iron he'll smoke the blow on duns
You run errands, Primatene Mist is afraid of my lungs
Turn my channel, it'll blow your whole bench off the panel
Like eighty roman candles that backfired then slammed you
Every day is like a video shoot, check this shit
I take it back to Playboy, stash guns in whips
Picture afro picks, shish kabobs and dashikis
Thousands civil marched, raised their fists in early sixties

It took time for me to get my solo joint simply because RZA was going with whoever was the hottest at that particular moment. He just knew, we all knew, it was what it was. Like, okay, who was first, because they were the hottest at that time. Meth was on "Protect Ya Neck," he tore it up. And he tore that solo record (*Tical*) up. So all of us already knew. But I wouldn't have gone next anyway, because Dirty was the hottest next to Meth. Those two were the hottest guys in the group at that time.

I mean, we put that work in on *Cuban Linx*. I put the work in on it. Raekwon had a battery in my back. We were feeding off each other, just going at it. Like, as far as street shit. And it's not only just that. It's a chemistry. When you got a chemistry with somebody like that, like Jordan and Pippen. So that chemistry went really, really well. Because I could have done it with anybody in the Clan, but it might not have connected like that.

And RZA was just doing what made sense. Like, I'm not on the same label at this time either. We all had different deals. RZA had a Sony deal over there, so he had a chance to put me on Sony. And we didn't want to just all drop at the same time either. So I think after *Cuban Linx*, Genius dropped *Liquid Swords* at Geffen, then I hit with *Ironman*. So it was like I knew I was coming up. But we never really sat down and had a powwow over it. It was just like, okay, I'm getting beats, RZA's giving me these beats and shit. And he's playing shit, I'm picking them, and yeah, that's how we got like some of *Ironman*.

The funny part about the title is that I'm not really a comics fan. One day, me and Rae was shopping, and I bought a shirt. That shirt became my Toney Starks shirt. Mind you, it didn't have Iron Man or Tony Stark on it or nothing like that. It's just that when I took on Ironman, I threw that shirt on, and I said, "Yo, this shit makes me feel like I'm Toney Starks or something." That was my Toney Starks shirt. And that's how all that Ironman shit came together.

At the time, I wasn't even sure that was going to be the name of the album. I had to make a decision, what should I name it? The first album was going to be *Ironman* or *Supreme Clientele*. Dake said *Ironman*, RZA said *Ironman*, some of my other friends said *Ironman*. I ain't asked everybody, but I think Lerisa said *Ironman*, and so did somebody else. So I was like, I'm coming off with Tony Starks. I'm after Raekwon. "Yo, *Ironman* should be the name of the album," and so *Supreme Clientele* was the next one.

Ironman and *Supreme Clientele* records

But around that time, it was just kind of dark. Because I couldn't even really write the way I wanted to write. It got dark. My best friend got locked up. The diabetes started taking its toll. I started losing a bunch of weight. I didn't know how to control it, I wasn't really checking my sugar like that. You know, I'm a young nigga and shit. So I didn't really know like, damn, I got to check my sugar and make sure it's all under there. Watch what you eat, and this and that. It just was like, in the summertime, you're recording all this other shit like that. So shit is just heavy on you. When you got diabetes, it'll make you weak. You get dizzy, it fucks with your eyes, just throws you off and shit like that.

> "And then, on top of that, you're losing weight. If you look at the 'Triumph' video, I'd lost mad weight by that time. So my neck got smaller, everything. Because when you're a diabetic, your sugar level be so high you start pissing all over the place. And I pissed out everything, bro. I pissed out so much fucking water. It's like every five minutes you peeing if your sugar is not controlled."

That's what you're seeing in the "Triumph" video when I'm like, "Yo, my neck was all little." You look at that video, then look at the "Ice Cream" video, it's two different versions of me. I was at my weakest around that time. Even when I did "Cobra Clutch," when I was mighty healthy and all that, I was still fucked up. With the diabetes and shit. It took me time to get and catch it, to really understand what's going on here. And shit like that. And I know because I could see it in my face on how tired I was doing the photo shoot for the album cover for *Supreme Clientele*. I was really fucking tired. When it's heavy on you, it makes you don't even want to stand up or tie your fucking shoe, or nothing like that. You don't want to do nothing. All you want to do is just sleep. So when I did the photo shoot, and I'm doing the dumb shit because I'm still smoking weed and all that. That's making me even more tired.

I felt bad for losing all that weight. I felt like niggas was looking at me like . . . And one thing about your brother, man, it's like a nigga could look fucked up and you know I lost weight. I was fucked up, and it was pretty obvious just by looking at me, but not one of my niggas ever came to me and asked was I all right. Like, "What's wrong with you?" Like "Yo, what's wrong? You all right? You're losing a lot of weight, man."

We got to start telling each other that shit. Now that I think about it today, it didn't come to my mind back then. I was glad they didn't ask me back then, because I probably would have felt even more fucked up. Damn, it looked like I might be dying out here. But now, like right now, when I look back, we got to do that to each other to try to help each other. We don't say nothing. Even with Dirt smoking all that crack and shit, niggas wasn't stepping into him like that. They wasn't stepping to him to try to be like, "Yo, fuck that. Yo, listen up." Niggas just letting the nigga just do what he got to do. And I don't think that's fair, but that's on another note.

The usual street shit was still going down then, too. Because you always got street shit. I remember one time I had beef with these niggas on Staten Island. I was going to the studio, so I got the Delfonics with me. Remember the Delfonics? It's a soul group. So I got them with me, they in the back of the van, like a fifteen-passenger. I'm in a Land Rover with my cousin and this other dude. And I got the gun on me. And so as I'm going to the studio, we had to get on the expressway to make it down over to Bay Street and the studio, which was called Mystic Studio.

So I got the Delfonics following me. I just so happened to see these kids getting on the expressway, and these niggas, they looking at me through the rearview mirror, and they laughing and shit. Like looking at me, so they're jumping in front of me. Wherever we turning, they turning, playing games. They in front of me, riding slow. They get off the exit. They in front, moving real slow.

I'm like, "Yo, I'm going to kill one of these niggas right now." I had the gun on me. So them niggas was doing a bunch of bullshit. They still riding slow, and dragging it out and all that. So as soon as they was about to make the turn to go their way, I just stuck my hand out the window and just let off like seven shots at these motherfuckas. Yo, I broke the back window, all that shit.

So we peel off. They turn around and start trying to chase us and shooting back at us. But I got the Delfonics with me. They older men, they're in the van behind me, watching all this shit go down.

"We're just flying down the street, and them niggas is trying to catch up. They shooting and shit, too. Like, I'm like, 'Yo, make this turn, make that turn, make that turn.' Boom. So they didn't follow us where we had to go. But it was crazy."

So when I got to the studio with the Delfonics. I had to apologize. "Yo, I'm sorry, man. I'm sorry." But they was like, "No, don't worry about it. No, no, no." They wasn't scared, because they from Philly. Philly don't play that shit neither. They was grown men. But they was like, "Damn, something told me to bring my knife. Something told me to bring my . . ." I was like, "Oh shit." Because he kept on saying, "Something told me to bring my damn knife. Something told me to bring my knife."

So shit was just going on, real shit around when I was making *Ironman*. It was just dark. To me, the album is not as bright. Like, *Supreme Clientele* is bright. *Ironman* seems like it's darker. The spirit of the album, to me and how I envision it, is dark.

But the album cover is crazy. I like bright colors. My favorite color's red. I love white, I love purple. Yellow. I like bright colors. I like good colors. Bright colors make me feel alive. You can't put me in the studio with a dull-ass room, because there's no thoughts going to come up. Once you put me in there with a room that got that sky blue and yellow, and a little bit of purple over here and all that. And white. It's like, yo, these rhymes come to life. You don't get sleepy and shit.

I really don't like really dark, dark, like brown. I can't stand brown. Don't give me nothing brown. Because I always wound up getting in fights and all that shit. I broke my ankle in my brown Wallabees. I never threw on brown again. Even on TV I don't look good in brown. The only thing brown that looks good on me is my skin.

The vibe has got to be right. And people don't understand that. That's why the *Ironman* album cover is crazy, because I had all them colorful Wallies up there. And to me, I think that's the best album cover in rap, as far as to my eye. And I think it's because the fucking album cover was tranquilizing you. It's like it was throwing you in a fucking spell, because even sometimes when I might look at it, if it was a big poster, I'll fuck around and get lost in it. Like, "Damn, these fucking shoes." It was just the colors. Then at the same time, we had the right clothes on for it. Like, Cap had the fucking red and yellow windbreaker on. Red, yellow, and green. And Rae had the green jacket.

In fact, when we did *Cuban Linx*, Cap was just coming home. That's why he got on "Ice Cream." He got on two songs, "Ice Cream" and "Ice Water." When he just came home, our album was probably damn near mostly in the bag already. But I always looked at Cap as like how me and Rae was on it. Me and Rae was on a mission, and I always looked at Cap to be right there, to be that third man. And that's why I called both of them for the cover.

Not even just to sell records, like, "Yo bro, you on a lot of these songs here." You want be like, "I'm on yours. Yo, we got to shoot the cover and Cap, too." But I always looked at Cap like part of the team, even if other niggas ain't look at him like that, I always looked at him that way. And Cap knows he can never get that from me. I was always like, "Nah, nah, Cap is on this." I was fighting for Cap's equal pay. To get the same shit we all got.

And that's what type of guys we are. Coming from Staten Island, it was like, Park Hill, Cap, and them had all the fashion. But I always fell in love with colorful things. And that's what it was. So I seen my whole vision of me wearing the robes and Wallabees and big-truck jewelry.

RISE OF A KILLAH: Ghostface Killah

Rise of the Ironman

I seen that in me back in the '80s. When I was rhyming, I said, "One day I'ma be like this. This is how I'ma be."

Like, you had one guy that was selling mad drugs on Staten Island. His name was Dusty. I think he was from Guyana. He was like the richest nigga in the Hill. He might've been the richest motherfucker on Staten Island. But he'd have on FILA velours, colorful shirts, with like three or four or five big chains. With little pieces hanging from the bottom of it. Like, hanging down to his dick with a mouthful of gold with just nappy hair. It was like a nappy Afro. Wasn't even really combed. But it didn't matter, because you knew this man was special with what he was out there doing. But the way I seen him with the jewelry, because he didn't wear no robes, I'm like, "Watch, when I get on, that's me right there."

Everything that you see based on me and my career is what I have already seen in my mind, and what came to me like that. I seen myself before I became known, I got dusted one day. And I seen myself on stage with EPMD. This was maybe like five years before I got on. I'm like, "Damn, I already seen this already." It took me five years, but I seen it. So I knew it was coming. I just had to wait my time. And with the robes and everything, it was like, yo, I was wearing robes, getting dusted, back in my projects, back before I was on in '88. It was like maybe the dust told me to throw on a fucking robe, a bathrobe that was in my house.

I remember, me and my man, my best friend, and it's like, yo, smoke that red devil, got dusted. I had the robe and that was it. So now it's like, damn, I get the robe. I have all this jewelry. Then I'm in front of a million people with just rhyming. And I got a mask on. It's like what the fuck more else you could ask for in rap?

The only reason I took the mask off because it was hard for me to breathe while rhyming. You can't wear a fucking stocking cap over your face for an hour, hour and a half, while you on stage rhyming. But at that time, I didn't know nobody to make me a nice decent mask where I would've kept the mask on, and I probably would've revealed my face like twenty or twenty-five years later. Like, yo, and that's it. "Oh shit. This that nigga right there?" And on it like that. And then I just added the robes to it and some Wallabees. And then I became a superhero.

My first piece was that Gucci link I mentioned earlier, the one that got snatched. I used to go down to Albee Square Mall and get me some fronts and shit. But then as the later years came on this rap shit, there was the Jesus head from when I did the "Ice Cream" video.

Yo, honey dip, summertime fine, Jheri dripping
Seen you on Pitkins with a bunch of chickens how you cliquing?
I kept shooting strong notes as we got close
She rocked rope, honey throat smelling like Impulse
Your whole shell baby's wicked like Nimrod
Caught me like a freshwater scrod, or may I not be God?
Attitude is very rude, boo, crabby like seafood
It turns me on like Vine's Cee Allah Rule
They call me Starky Love, hon, check the strategy
By any means, Shirley Temple curls was done by Billie Jeans
Black Mrs. America, your name is Erica, right true
Lazy eyeball, small feet, six shoe
Caramel complexion, breath smelling like cinnamon
Excuse me, hon, the Don mean no harm, turn around again
Goddamn, backyard's banging like a Benzi
If I was jiggy, you'd be spotted like Spuds McKenzie
I'm high-powered, put Adina Howard to sleep
Yo, pardon, that bitch been on my mind all week
But, uh, back to you, Maybelline queen, let's make a team
You can have anything in this world except C.R.E.A.M.
So what you wanna do? What you wanna do?
Let's go ahead and walk these dogs and represent Wu

At that time, it would cost, I think, like five or six thousand dollars at that time on Canal Street. I was with Steve Rifkind, we was down there, copped that. Copped that, and then after that, it just came to the next bigger shit. Like, oh shit, a big, big eagle on my arm because you know that's when I was like the Wonder Woman bracelet. But this shit was like Shazam.

Ghostface with globe bracelet

For "All That I Got Is You," I was at one of RZA's houses, out of town. And, you know, he had a bunch of land and shit. And we just on the land, and he playing beats and shit. So we just in there, he was playing me a bunch of beats for *Ironman*, and that's one of the beats that stuck out to me. So I'm like, "Yo, I want that one. Give me this one right here." So then I took it home, and then I just wrote to it.

For me, writing verses come from wherever your mind is at—like at that time it wasn't a story for me. If the beat says it tells the story, then that's what I had to do. But I really had no angle. What is that angle? Have you heard of brothers like really freestyling, freestyling and just rhyming around like abstract, then that's what it was. Sometimes a beat would be the call for a certain thing, a certain like, "All That I Got Is You," was taken off my childhood because that's what I heard.

It just came from the beat that makes you say what you say over it. I mean, the beat is the most important, to me, besides the lyrics. They go together. But a lot of times, the beat will grab you to tell what you say. That's why, to me, it's like always the beat first. Because it will put you in that mood like, what you got to say? If the shit is an R & B beat, you write R & B. If the shit sound real sad, you write real sad.

That's where "Wildflower" came from. I got my heart broke. I didn't like that pain, 'cause that was like my first girlfriend. She kinda cheated on me and stuff. So I just carried that with me, and eventually I put it out with words. She ain't even gonna know. I did tell her, "Yo, you broke my heart." I didn't tell her "Wildflower" was based on you made me write that shit.

I know I have an old soul and I know I'm in tune. I have an old soul because I'd rather rhyme off old soul music than what I would do to the music just right now regular. I get a kick out of old shit. A lot of old '70s shit. If I had the choice, I'd rather you give me those beats, and y'all could keep the other shit.

"All That I Got Is You," it sounded like the shit I talked on it. "Dwelling in the past, flashbacks when I was young / Whoever thought that I'd have a baby girl and three sons?" And I just took that line and connected everything from that line right there, because a lot of times, your first line would lead to a masterpiece. It all starts with the first line. That's why nowadays, I might write like three verses. Three, eight bars, just to get that first start, because that's what's very important.

I laid it down, because I go off of wherever the beat takes you. The emotion of it. It sounded dope the way it came on anyway. But it just took me to my childhood. You know sometimes people, artists, the beat speaks to you. It'll tell you whether it's a murder. Or it'll tell you like, yo, it feels like a good day. That one just felt like some type of pain. Childhood pain. Just growing up and all that. It put me in that mood to talk about my childhood, my upbringing. When fifteen of us were in a three-bedroom apartment, roaches everywhere. I'm probably one of the first people to go ahead and go deep inside those realms there, without really feeling embarrassed about where I came from. Like I'm talking about being used to spending food stamps, and going to my friend's house, asking could we borrow some food? We broke.

So it took me back from looking at all that shit, looking at how my mother was, how she was raising us. And what was going on in the house. And shit like that. Where I just laid it all out, that I could at that time. And it was so much truth to it, that people, they gravitated to it and seemed to like it.

Then we got Mary J. Blige on it, and she just wrapped it up. We was in Mystic Studio on Staten Island. I laid my part down first, then she came into the studio to do her hook after the song was done. She sung it after my verse. And she murdered it. She absolutely murdered it. Mary was real good to work with.

Now the concept for the video—me playing piano out on the street mixed with clips of growing up on Staten Island—came from the producer. So I decided to bring my son and put him in there when he was real little. We was out in California. That was in Universal Studios, up there where they got all the fake houses and buildings and where they shoot a lot of TV shows. So we just knocked that out.

But Mary couldn't do the video. I guess her label at that time was just fronting on her, or something. She apologized for it later on when I seen her again. So we had to put Tekitha in. I mean, I was going off of what RZA was saying, because that was his artist. So he want to stick his artist in there to try to sing the song over. And I was young at that time. If it was me now, no disrespect, Tekitha my sister and all that, but I would've tried to put Monica or somebody like her on it. To bring more star power, how it would've just came off with like a Mary J.

Blige. But I thought about that afterward. But while that was taking place early, it didn't cross my mind like that. When you young, you still got to learn the business. By that time, I was twenty-six. So it was like I was only three years wet in the game.

At that time, I didn't think it was going to be the kind of song it turned out to be. I played it for Raekwon and shit. He was like, "Oh, shit. Yo, that shit crazy." Like, you know, they just thought it was good rap. I mean, I didn't think it was anything really special, when I just was doing what I do. I didn't think it was really special to me, doing that record, or doing that album.

That whole album was all in the moment, because I would take the beats and try to write to all of them, and try to get things done by a certain time. That's why I said I don't do deadlines now. Because even with that album, I had to hurry up and rush a few songs.

The funny thing is that looking back on *Ironman* today, I'm not satisfied with it. It would have been more colorful and juicy, like where I left off with Raekwon's shit, and that's why when it dropped, I wasn't too happy with it. It was cool, and it was my first one, but I had Nas right there coming out at the same time. And it's like, "Damn, I wanted to come out and compete with these niggas, because these niggas are my peers." But I couldn't get up in there like that.

I was going through too much shit. My mind wasn't where it needed to be. *Ironman* wasn't an outlet for me to escape those problems I was having. I had to do what I had to do in the midst of being under all that pressure. If it was an outlet for me, I would've done more on it than what I planned to do. Like even if you catch the joint RZA did with Inspectah Deck and Masta Killa, "Assassination Day." I'm not on that song because I couldn't think. I couldn't ride the beat. I couldn't even think of shit. So I just put them on the song and left it there. It's on my album, but I'm not on that song. So that was just a filler right there.

And it was frustrating. It stressed me out. It was really solid for its time and shit. But it could have been way better, a lot better. Like, if I hadn't rushed it, I would've had way more lyrics on there and a lot more elements, like beats and shit. A lot of those rhymes would've come out different. Probably more detailed and I would have said more shit. But I had to make that deadline, and the deadline was October.

Even so, I didn't think *Ironman* would have this impact, because I wasn't too wrapped up in it. I'm grateful. I'm truly blessed to here twenty-five years later from my first joint when I was like twenty-six years old. A lot of people don't get to make it like that and still keep going.

CHAPTER 8

ONE

[Chorus: Ghostface Killah]
Ayo, the Devil planted fear inside the black babies
Fifty cent sodas in the hood, they going crazy
Dead meat placed on the shelves, we eat cold cuts
Fast from the hog y'all and grow up (Grow up)

[Verse 1: Ghostface Killah]
Ayo, we at the weedgate, waitin' for Jake
We want eight ravioli bags, two thirsty villains yelling bellyaches
Heavyweight rhyme writers hittin' the grass
Stash the right bitch, pull out his kite from this white bitch
Talkin' 'bout, "Dear Ghost, you the only nigga I know
Like when the cops come, you never hide your toast"
Guests started mashing, CVL, Ice Water battalion
Past tense place to gold caskets
Dru Hill bitches, specialist loungin' at the mosk
Suede cufy, Rabbi come dig up a dentist
Rhymes is made of garlic, never in the target
When the NARC's hit, rumor is you might start to spit
You nice Lord, sweet daddy Grace, wind lifted

On the dance floor, mangos is free followed by Ghost
Dug behind monument cakes, we never half-baked
Alaskan, cess-capade, pushin' new court dates
Trauma, hands is like candy canes, lay my balls on ice
The branches in my weed be the vein {"one"}
Swimsuit issue, darts sent truly from the heart, boo, I miss you
See daddy rock a wristful
Moder-en slave God, graveyard spells, fog your goggles
Layin' like needles in the hospital
Five steps to conquer, Ax Vernon debt, big ass whistle
Ziplock your ear, here thistle

[Verse 2: Ghostface Killah]
Ayo, crash through, break the glass, Tony with the goalie mask
That's the past, heavy ice Rollie laying on the dash
Love the grass, cauliflower hurting when I dumped the trash
Sour mash served in every glass up at the Wally Bash
Sunsplash, autograph blessing with your name slashed
Backdraft, four-pounders screaming with the pearly ash
Children fix the contrast as the sound clashes

Mrs. Dash, sprinkle with her icicle eyelash
Ask Cappa Pendergrass for backstage passes
Special guest, no more Johnny Blaze, Johnny Mathis
Acrobat, run up on that Love Jones actress
Distract the cat while I'm high, sugar, get a crack at this
Dicking down Oprah, jump rope, David Dinkins
Watch the black mayor of DC hit the mocha
Tangerine sofa, two super soakers in the Rover
Hit the sports bar, tell a young lady to bend over
Meditated yoga, Paddle Ball, dancing with the vulture
Castor Troy laying for Travolta
Yo, switch the lingo, five-nine-seventy
God glow, seven fifteen four be ebony

During this time I went to Benin, in Africa, for several months.

I went there in '97 with a friend that I met at one of my shows, my man Elijah. He said, "Yo . . . I go back and forth to Africa." He was dealing with these diamonds and all that other shit. I said, "Yo, I want to go there." He said, "Yo, let's go for a couple of weeks." And that's what I did.

We went to West Africa. In Benin, next to Nigeria. I stayed in the village, not in a popular area. The village was poor, and I know that's complicated in itself. Knowing where your next meal's going to come from and stuff like that. But they don't got to face the things we was facing. You ain't got to worry about guns in that part of Africa. I wasn't in the city, I was probably like an hour or two from the city. But they was happy. They was poor as the fuck, but they was happy. There wasn't no murders. I think the one person who died there that year was somebody that got hit by a car.

I'm in the village where they cook outside with no stoves. They wash their clothes, they cook outside, you got to take your shit outside. You had to do all that, and you had to bathe outside. I stayed at the only house that had a TV, like a small black-and-white TV, nothing big. You got to fix the hanger on it, then turn it. Because the contrast be like, "Shhh." And the only house that had light. It might've been one house that lit up, that we got the electricity from somewhere. And that was it. Everybody else had their huts, their homes and stuff like that, made the same way. It was dark all around. No streetlights, no nothing.

Not moving around the house because it wasn't a house. They didn't even have a roof. They had to put up a metal wall just to cover the fucking roof on the house. I think it was one light in there or something like that. I had a candle where I was at in another room, though.

And I used to be like, "Shit. I got to go to the bathroom at three or four in the morning." There ain't no streets. You just in a bush somewhere. So you got to go to bathroom three in the morning. You're going to have to walk out the house. I don't care if you got to do number two or whatever, you're going to be out there by yourself. They had a little brick wall where nobody could see where you're pissing or shitting. So you go in there, there's a hole in the floor where you got to squat, go ahead and take your little number twos or whatever or take a piss and stuff like that. It had a little water. You pour the water on your hand. Soap was right there. And wash your hands while you pouring the water.

We ate. They would get me fresh eggs from the chickens that laid them. They cooked me breakfast. Just some eggs. So it wasn't really like eggs and sausages, egg sandwiches. I see them take peanuts. Step on a bunch of peanuts, right? And make peanut butter sticks out of them. They'd flatten them out and get the oil off the peanuts they was flattening. And they'll take that oil and that'll be peanut butter oil. And then they'll roll a stick with their hand. Roll the crushed peanuts up with their hand and make peanut butter sticks and go sell them for nickels.

> "Five o'clock in the morning, you got the men, the boys got to chop the trees down. The women had to wash clothes. Had to go wash, had to cook, clean, do all that shit like that. Soon as you hear that rooster crow at five . . . 'Cock a doodle doo.' They got to get up and get going."

It became a time where I had to take my clothes off because I felt funny wearing my street clothes amongst they shit. I had to go ahead and go buy one of the suits they had. The little dashikis. Was wearing slippers. No haircut. I was out there looking like Moses and shit like that. But you know what? It was good. That was probably the best experience I ever had in my life because I went back down to nature. I was free.

It was an experience. Black people is from Africa. We're from that region, Benin, Nigeria. I even took a little bit of the dirt just to bring it back. Like, "Man, this is where I come from exactly." Like, "I'm in Africa." It really felt like Africa. Like how you say it, how does it sound. And that's how you looked at it. "I'm in Africa right now. This is Africa." Like, "Holy shit."

So yeah, it was an experience. The stars at night was heavy. Like I used to see stars like that when we was little, especially when I was little, my early teens and all that when the stars used to be heavy. But I hadn't seen stars in a long time. It seemed like it was fucking hundreds and thousands, billions of 'em. It was flooded, all those stars. Big ones, little ones, bright ones, baby ones. It was crazy. In the U.S., I was always wondering where the fuck did the stars go. I guess it was the pollution that was hiding all the goddamn stars.

It was totally different over there. I learned we was blessed in America. They was blessed there, too. But you know what? They had really no money. And money didn't really count. To get whatever you need, it's like a struggle. We sit here, we can order a pizza pie, right? We could order a pizza pie and throw away the crust. When you got people over there, pay a dime for that crust. That'll go in the garbage and go in there and eat that crust. Certain people. Not the ones I was out with over there. You got certain people that'll go do that.

And I realized, yo man, it's like, we got it. So I left all my clothes there. Even when I went to the schools, it started raining and all the kids ran home. Why? Because they had no roof over the school. So what I did, I sent back money for them to go ahead and put a roof over this school. And to this day I still take care of them same children out there. You feeding a bunch of children that's there like that. You send it back to them.

It's like a lot of shit I do, I don't tell a lot of people, but every month I take care of people over there like that. Everybody just so they can eat. If somebody passes away, I'm right here to help bury them. That's just what it is. That's how God made me. I don't got to go ahead and blast the shit around. "Yo, I did this for the people." It's like, no, I don't spread that. And it's like, I'm telling you my experience when I touched the motherland.

Our brains and the way we think . . . since we're not at home, we might never be able to get to that capacity because this ain't your land. You know what I mean? This ain't your land. So that feeling that you supposed to feel and the way you supposed to really think, you're not connected. You been stolen and brought here, so you really can't understand this land. That's why things might not even go right for Latinos and the Hispanics and all that stuff because this ain't their fucking land either.

Now don't get me wrong, it's okay that we here and it's like that. That's just how it went, God did whatever he did. But as far as the connection, you could really never have a connection with a place that's not your place. It's almost like you're coming into the house. When you gone, you sleep in the hotels, right? But when you get to your bed-bed, that's your bed. Africa is my bed. If you was a white person or whatever, Europe might be your bed, or America might be your bed. You felt closer to everything there. For my spirit, I felt closer to God, right there in Africa. Black people in America, we'd probably be discombobulated and be off, because we're not connected to this place. We're not connecting, spiritually.

The Indians might have more of a connection here than maybe the Blacks and the whites. Even a white man or an Indian is probably more connected to this place. Whoever was here before us, because this is where you're from. We're not from here, we were still slaves that was brought over here, to get and put that to work. We have a tendency of forgetting that. When you're not connected to your land, my belief is it'll have you off-balance a little bit and have you thinking another way.

"I could walk out my house in America, and it's cool because I'm used to it, but it's a different feeling when you know your soul and your spirit is connected to a place right here. In America, all I know is America, so you come up with it as you come up with it. This could be the reason why a lot of us is all fucked up. Hispanics and Blacks and all this other shit, we're fucked up, because we're not really connected here. We don't even really know how to treat each other, because we're off, we're totally off."

The people that live here that was here before us, they probably could feel a spirit, like I felt in Africa. I felt the spirit when I was there, I felt connected. It was home. This is where I come from. And I was so excited to go because I was going to go there. I'm just happy that I'm going back to the motherland. As soon as the plane touched down, I'm here. I'm here, but you don't know until you go back because once you get there, everything starts coming in your head. You start thinking about slavery, how he took us from here. How he did that. Damn, we're fucking, we spoiled, we got the luxury and all that other shit over here. These are my brothers and my sisters here, they don't even know. They might not even know, but somewhere we are still connected, and just the energy from what the earth gives you from being, if you're from that region, the energy from the earth, if you're in tune with yourself, you can feel that shit. Damn and it's a good feeling, you just feel good, happy.

> "New York City is my home because that's where I came from, but I've been living in different places and stuff like that. New York is the mecca for everything. This is what keeps America going. It's New York City. If it wasn't for New York City, a lot of this shit wouldn't be going on, rap music, a lot of shit. The stock market, pizza, every fucking thing."

I've been in New York for many years. I was born in New York. There are places I go to that I feel comfortable in just spiritwise, like Atlanta, I feel comfortable in Atlanta. My spirit feels comfortable in Florida. My spirit feels comfortable in Hawaii. My spirit feels comfortable in North Carolina. I love Chicago, too. Chicago is a good city and Philly is a good city. Places where my spirit feels like that, that means I can live there. It's just certain feelings about a place and shit.

And I wrote one rhyme when I was in Africa. On *Supreme Clientele*, the first rhyme on there. Now, I don't want the fans to get it twisted. I only wrote one verse there.

Something said, "Yo, make a record with words that really don't mean nothing but you just saying a bunch of words that just sound good." And that's how I did "Nutmeg" and people don't understand it. People think I'm dropping a lot of science in there. Try to figure it out and this and that, but it was just words I put together because I had no music. I didn't have to have music there. All I had to play is a beat in my head and just wrote down whatever I wrote down. That's what I did. I wrote the beat with no music in my head. All the stars was out, and I'm in the village, so I just thought of a style I could run to that don't mean nothing. The words just rhyme, but it's really no meaning to any of it. I'm just putting words together that make it just sound good, that don't make no sense. And it's funny because people try to decipher the words, and it's like, "Nigga, I don't even know what the fuck is happening here."

It was the sound that I was creating that I thought, let me do something nobody never did before, and that was it. That was how I got "Nutmeg." Let me do a style that somebody never did before. People, they'll be trying to figure out what I'm talking about, trying to decipher it. There's nothing to decipher. It's just words. And that's how I got "Nutmeg." "Nutmeg" and "One" and all that shit, I just put words together that really didn't mean nothing, but it sounded dope over the beat when I laid it down. For the African people, I don't know if they're ever going to read this and be like, "Holy shit, that was that."

But I did that and I made *Supreme Clientele*. But if I had never went there, I probably would never have had the idea. If I hadn't been there at that point in time, there'd be a different song starting off *Supreme Clientele*.

And that style influenced other rappers as well. That's how MF Doom got his style. He told me that one day: "You know, I got that from you. The abstract it's just like off the wall shit." When I wrote that rhyme in Africa, the "Nutmeg" shit, it didn't really make no sense. And then here go Doom with the shit that didn't really make no sense neither. So him telling me that was an honor. Like, "Oh, shit." And I never really knew it. You know. In rap, it's like we all just take from whatever we find along the way. But he was the type that he told me personally.

I came back from Africa, and even on the plane I was sweating a little bit. While I was out there, I felt fine. And when I got on that plane, I just felt a little like getting hot, sweating a little bit and . . . I came back and I remember I started getting weaker. I had a show, the next day when I came back. It was close, though, for me to return for it.

And I think it was in Baltimore with the Clan, and I felt so weak. So I go to the doctors and they sent me back home. Like, "Nah, just drink fluids and this and that and a bunch of fluids and whatever." I tried, all that. It didn't work. So as days went on, I started getting weaker and weaker, until I couldn't even walk. And when I couldn't walk, it was time to go to the hospital again. I forgot what hospital it was, but then I know I had to go to Long Island to my doctor Stewie. I went to him and then he sent me to another hospital there.

I was in there for three weeks, maybe a month. Because it was like, "Wow." It was on. I didn't know where I was at, exactly what year it was. I'm saying like, "I'm not signing autographs," and stuff like that. It was crazy. And then at that time I had asked, because they wanted the spinal tap, and RZA was saying, "No." I called him. He was like, "No. Don't take the spinal tap because you can mess around and get paralyzed, fucking with your spine and all that shit like that." But these guys had to take the spinal tap so they could know what it was. I'm glad I didn't listen to him that time, because I probably would have been finished.

So when they found out what it was—turns out I came back with malaria—because they never asked me did I leave the country? They never asked me that. So I was in there for a minute. Lost mad weight. I couldn't even walk. They had to put a catheter in my penis so I could piss. All that shit. And I had to get my weight up again. That was rough—it was a time I'll never forget.

CHAPTER 9

WU-TANG FOREVER

Yo, up in the M.G.M. coked up, psych!
Six niggas walked in flashing they gems piece
Aight, one dark-skinned nigga, fifty-six-inch rope
Wrapped around twice, smash the Gilligan boat with ice
They threw sign language, ordered hot coffee wit' a danish
Relax, whispered they, "Rap entertainers"
Had Lizzy on, two Japanese birds with furs look good, Kid
Laid back, handling hors d'ourves
It's like round three, we too black for BET
You memorize the 1 to 40? I'm at the 19th degree
If a civilized person doesn't perform his duty, what shall be done?
Pardon me, God, that nigga got a gun bulging out his sweatpants
Check out his stance
See the side of his grill? Look like my cousin Lance
Left hand, rocky Guess watch, yo, I think I did his Clarks
He wanted crush bone leather with the strings dark
Now I remember, he from Bear Mountain
He and Mitch Greene shot the fair one near the water fountain
Seventh round, Chavez bleeding from his right ear
Yo, keep your eye on that same nigga from right here

Popcorn spilling all on Liz Claiborne
Ghost had the fly Gucci mocks wit' no socks on
Seen Deion Sanders in the back with the phat fur on
Working them hoes with the fly Wu shirts on
Mixed drink session, dun, pour me some more
Chef leathered down, blinking at Chante Moore
Tenth round, Chavez tearing 'em down
Sweet Pea, get ya shit off
It's like blacks against the Germans, getting hit off
Smooth and them walked in, Brownsville representing
They sent a bottle over, autograph blessing
Chef, pull out the doo-doo, twist the dank – pink noodles
Yo, about to roll one, matter fact, twist two of those
Yo, they wound up stopping the fight
Steels took a point away from Chavez
Rematch scheduled on October 9th
Rematch scheduled on October 9th

Wu-Tang Forever

In '97, it was time to do *Wu-Tang Forever*, the full-crew follow-up to *36 Chambers*. The last album we dropped all together was in '93. It had been four years, and it was time. We basically knew the second album was coming. We going to go to LA and write and record that, and be out there for a couple of months, and finish the job and come back.

Doing *Forever* was a lot different than *36*. We was more in our element now. We got a chance to move around and stuff like that. Just moving around, me seeing things, being over there. I think before we got to the Mulholland Drive mansion, when we stayed in a big house in the Oakwoods. We had a house up there and all that. We was all in there just banging out, writing tracks. But we'd go down to the Amercayan Studios over there on Lankershim Boulevard every day.

> "This was the first time all ten of us were together in one place for an extended period of time. Even on tour, it wasn't like all of us were crammed up in the same hotel room. And because the place was huge, everybody had space. We also didn't have a studio there, so we weren't recording where we were living. Music was still on all the time, though. At that time, it was like CDs and shit like that. So you might have a radio, put it in and probably play it there in the corner or whatever the case is."

And then, studio time. We would go down to the studio and just write. And then when you finished your verse, you lay it down and shit. So it was tight like that. We really never beefed over anything, like a beat or whatever, or I never saw it. You make it, you make it. If you don't make it, you don't make it. That's on you. Whether you was writing, probably taking too long to write or whatever and shit like that. Me, I like to write at home. I like to write indoors, away from the studio, so I could just come and just lay my shit down, because, like I said, I don't like being rushed.

To me, it don't really matter whether I'm collaborating with someone or when I'm writing on my own. But if I gotta rush to do something, then I'd rather do it by myself. I don't want to rush, but my flow is what it is. Probably everybody in the crew—me and Genius might be the ones that might take all day. I second-guess a lot of my shit. Like sometimes I might just think it's right, but then I might hear the next man's version and be like, "Damn, I could have came crazier." But I did try to finish it just in time so that I give it to you. I'm almost like a good counterpuncher. Like, if it was boxing, you try to come at me, and I see that punch coming at my head, I'm gonna come back at you twice as hard.

But as far as timing, if I'm on the clock, I'd rather write by myself. But, when me and Rae is in there, bouncing off each other, that's fun, too. Because all he do is open up my mind. We opened up each other's minds in there like that. The part where my mind wasn't open, it's like, "oh shit, okay." He'd fuck around and spark that. So now it's like, oh shit. Then from that comes more of the shit, and you just try to run with it.

So a lot of times I would come in there, lay down my rhymes, and do shit. Now as far as writing at the time, I wasn't really in that frame of mind, because of the diabetes and all that. But even while all of this is going on, somehow I still was able to create one of my best, if not my best verse ever, on "Impossible":

Call an ambulance, Jamie been shot, word to Kimmy
Don't go, son, nigga, you my motherfucking heart
Stay still, son, don't move, just think about Keeba
She'll be three in January, your young God needs ya
The ambulance is takin' too long
Everybody get the fuck back, excuse me, bitch, gimme your jack
1-7-1-8, 9-1-1, low battery, damn
Blood comin' out his mouth, he bleedin' badly
Nahhh, Jamie, don't start that shit
Keep your head up, if you escape hell, we gettin' fucked up
When we was eight, we went to Bat Day to see the Yanks
In '69, his father and mines, they robbed banks
He pointed to the charm on his neck
With his last bit of energy left, told me rock it with respect
I opened it, seen the God holdin' his kids
Photogenic, tears just burst out my wig
Plus he dropped one

Oh shit, here come his old Earth with no shoes on
Screamin', holdin' her breasts with a gown on
She fell and then lightly touched his jaw, kissed him
Rubbed his hair, turned around, the ambulance was there
Plus the blue coats, Officer Lough, took it as a joke
Weeks ago he strip-searched the God and gave him back his coke
Bitches yellin', Beenie Man swung on Helen
In the back of a cop car, Dirty Tasha tellin'
But suddenly, a chill came through, it was weird
Felt like my man, was cast out my heaven now we share
Laid on the stretcher, blood on his Wallys like ketchup
Deep like the Paul assassination with a sketch of it
It can't be, from Yoo-hoo to Lee's
Second grade humped the teachers, about to leave
Finally, this closed chapter comes to an end
He was announced, pronounced dead, y'all, at 12:10

I remember writing it. I remember laying it down. I had to come back to it—I had to do it one day, and then come back and finish writing it the next day. I didn't just lay it down all at once. You know, certain beats bring shit out. So when I heard that beat, it just brought it out at that time. I didn't know it was going to come out like that, but it just came out.

So my mind was like, when I'm writing a movie, you know what I mean? It's like, I see things so vividly, and this is how I saw "Impossible" when I did that verse. And the beat was so theatrical to me because it just sounded deep. So I'm playing with it when it starts to intensify and up, and it starts to come down. I wrote the rhyme like that, like, okay, yeah, it's going up, it's come down. So I blew it like that, and it just came out and I just stayed on that topic. I just told a story. One of my baby's mother's brothers got killed. I didn't see the murder go down, but I saw how she left the house and ran downstairs at the moment and stuff like that. I was just explaining, put a little bit of that inside that verse. It wasn't even based on a whole true event. Just a couple of bars maybe, but the thing was just in my head. Just made it up.

So certain music will bring it out, because I look at music like females when I pick my beats, because I like fat chicks. You got to know how to ride that shit. When you get that, when you get that nice white chick, it's like, yo, you got to just pound it. You got to represent. Sometimes I go for some time. Sometimes, your dick might not get up for the bitch, but she's still a bad bitch. We all know what it is. It's almost like the same thing writing it, where you got to come back and go at it again. I didn't write it right the first time. But let me come back to that shit again. And then you might just tackle it the right way.

That's how I write my music. I always look at my music like that. Like, if it's a beat and the beat is juicy, that's like a bad chick to me. So if a dude said you have a beat that's half-ass, you might not really do that good on it, because the track sucks. But you might have to do it anyway. It's like taking one for the team.

Now when I can't get into a song for some reason or whatever, now I've been in there for so long I know how to get ahead and I know how to move around it. You know how to be like, okay, don't force it. Okay, come back to it, come back to it. Sometimes you lose inspiration.

Like, a lot of the times, back then, I used to love to write with Biggie, Knives, and all the great mob beefs. It was dope back then. It was a bunch of writers (Biggie, Jay-Z, Nas, Prodigy, etc.) and it was like, okay, cool, Jay-Z's doing his thing. Back in the day hip hop was inspiring to me. Oh, you got this album. You got that album. Oh, the album is crazy. It's crazy, all the songs on it are crazy. Now, it's not like that no more. It's right now it's about putting one song, probably just one song out. People don't even care about your album. It's like, damn, I don't put sixteen fucking tracks, put twelve to sixteen songs on here. And I created like a masterpiece and nobody gets to hear it, they just get to hear one song or something like that.

Now they don't even use that like that. And a lot of my albums that was real street albums was not really the side projects that I did. Like, I did a couple of side projects. *36 Seasons*, *Twelve Reasons to Die*. *Sour Soul* with BadBadNotGood, and a couple other ones. *Wu-Massacre* and all this other shit like that.

But when I'm doing my *Fishscale* and *The Pretty Toney Album* and *Bulletproof Wallets*, *Ghostdini: The Wizard of Poetry* and all that shit, it's me lining all that shit up like that. It's me putting them into order, doing the audit, sitting there, trying to figure out whether the album did good or not. That's just me. I like to put the songs in order and make 'em neat, which sounds good coming out, because an important thing about an album is try to find a vibe. That's why you can listen to *Supreme Clientele* and *Ironman* and not really skip through 'em. Just hear it all the way out because that's how I built it for you. That's how we did *Cuban Linx*. Me and Rae sat there with *Cuban Linx* and it was like, "Yo, no, no, put that first. Start that off. Yo, start it off hyper like that." So it was a system.

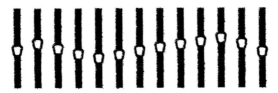

I threw mad verses around in the day. I never looked at myself as being perfect, because there's always room to make it better. I did "Impossible" in '97, so as you grow, you see things in your old music. I looked at *Fishscale* one time and was like, "I didn't even need all those tracks. Why the fuck I put a bunch of tracks on there when I could have just made it just nice and bulky, sitting up there like a pit bull just with eleven tracks strong, and just beat niggas in the head?"

So sometimes you don't need all that. But when you was coming, you thought you needed all that, sixteen tracks, a guy to be there like, "You do twelve, if you do fourteen . . ." Give him a bonus cut, and this and that. And so you learn as you go. So now when I look at some of the verses I did back in the day, yeah, I had a couple. "Impossible" was ill. "4th Chamber" (from *Liquid Swords*) was kind of ill. And I wouldn't have changed it.

The only man a ho wait for
Is the sky-blue Bally Kid, in '83 rocked Tale Lords
My Memorex performed tape decks, my own phone sex
Watch out for Haiti bitches, I heard they throw hex
Yo, Wu whole platoon is filled with raccoons
Corner-sittin' wine niggas sippin' Apple Boone
This ain't no white cartoon
'Cause I be duckin' crazy spades
The Kid hold white shit like blacks rock ashy legs
Why is the sky blue? Why is water wet?
Why did Judas rat to Romans while Jesus slept?
Stand up, you're out of luck like two dogs stuck
Ironman be sippin' rum out of Stanley Cups, unflammable
Noriega, aimin' nozzles, stay windy in Chicago
Spine-tingle, mind boggles
Kangols in rainbow colors, promoters try to hold dough
Gimme mine before Po wrap you up in so-and-so
I ran the Dark Ages, Constantine the Great, Henry the 8th
Built with Genghis Khan, the red suede Wally Don

What I got better at was probably some hooks. And, of course, more writing. It's just that my mind when I was doing those older projects—like for *Cuban Linx*, I was twenty-five, so my mind was open to more street shit at that time. Remember, we still had bricks, were still moving them and shit like that. I was still in the project with it. I was just seeing shit on the corner. Once you come off that corner, your mindset starts to change when you not doing these things you did twenty years ago. You just ain't doing it. So whatever lingo and all that shit I'm getting be from the niggas I'm around now, opposed to me out there just doing it.

So that's why I could understand when you could take Nas on *Illmatic*, because he was there. That's one of my best rappers ever in the world, ever, ever, ever, ever. He was in the projects right there, you could see it, you could hear it. "We was at the Candy Factory breaking the locks," when he said that shit right there, you could see it all, just running around. Even if he didn't do it, you could still see it. His mindset was still there, and it was like, okay, you was there with him because you was in the same shit. You was in the projects, too. Still running around and seeing shit, getting to Virginia and back, Philly and back, and all this other shit like that, just moving.

Now it's different. Now you just throwing grown-man rhymes around and he ain't in there like that. So it's not the same shit. When you grow, you grow. Jay wasn't rhyming about Basquiat and all that back in '96, '97. Now he knows the weird things in the art gallery. Yeah, he know those kind of names and shit. You grow, I'm not saying like everybody else, but you grow. Things don't stay the same. I became more closer into my Islam. I grew. I don't do the same thing I used to do. I'm much more wise. I'm much more connected spiritually to the Most High.

I've grown to the point where if I'm doing something really foul, it's going to hurt me. I'm going to feel bad. But like I told you before, even if I stole a book of matches from you, I would feel like, "Damn." I would feel fucked up. So if I got to feel fucked up in taking something from somebody, that means I shouldn't have did it. Back then I didn't give a fuck. So I'm growing like this, I know where I want to see myself. And a lot of things that I did I'm trying to correct now just as a man, just growing, your relationships and things in that nature and all that other shit like that.

Yeah man, you just grow, grow mentally. You try to take care of yourself physically. Because once your body passes a certain age it's like, "Okay, yo, you about to turn forty." Because when you hit fifty, the clock start going the other way now. You hit the midpoint at fifty and then the clock starts going this way like, "Oh, shit." So, yeah, man you start thinking. Like I said, I think differently. I don't think the same like back then.

> "Back then I could drink two 40-ounces and it's the ping go off. Now, I don't drink 40s no more. I don't even really drink no more. I might drink when the fight is on, or I got to go to a club, but that's it. Back then I used to drink every day, *Cuban Linx* and all that shit like that. So now I don't smoke, and I don't really drink like that."

So now I got to find it where it's coming from another place, a different place. And sometimes you need to open that door. You need that door to open up. I feel like weed and shit opens up the closed door. Sometimes you could just go ahead and go right in and shit like that. But I'm looking at the comparisons of when I did drink and write and now, when I sit at that table without it. And now the thoughts ain't coming as fast. But I still get it done, though, it just takes longer, sometimes it takes much longer.

I might get a block now and then, but I'll never, never really run out of lyrics because knowledge is infinite. The mind is infinite. There's always something to talk about. I know I'm going to be throwing rhymes around until I'm an old man, because that's what I just love to do. If Allah spares my life and gives me good health and long life and happiness, I'll be throwing them around like that. Even if I'm not recording, I got to write as an old man. And I'm already prepared for it, because if I got to talk about my cane, my false teeth, health care, grandchildren, I'm ready to do all that.

See, I'm a unique type of person. I can make certain things and swag it out, and just sound good. Like, "Yo, this is a sly old man right here." I will believe even if the Most High push me to seventy or eighty, the way I think, I would still think I could dust some of these little kids off.

I think if the Most High spares me, I think I'm going to be able to hang with these little dudes and go ahead and make music with them and be right there on the front line. Because they going to know Pops. They going to be calling me Pops by that time, "Yo, Pops, what up? Yeah, yeah, yeah, yeah. Yo, yo let me hear that dart shoot over here." Just like that or whatever. Let me see y'all little whippersnappers, what it's really about. And get in there and just do what it do.

Because it ain't like you a boxer and you get slower because you got punched in your head so many times. Now, when you dealing with this, if you don't got no Parkinson's and all that shit like that, and no other sicknesses come to fuck you up, I think you could go ahead and still throw this around. And I think in rap I think it will just lead to that, because what goes around comes around. And there's going to be a time when it starts coming back around in lyrics.

Some of the people that survive this, it's no disrespect to the new generation, but it's going to be a time when they going to have to be like, "What are you talking about now? Say something." Because everything ain't going to be just based on about a party and all this other shit like that. You got to have some type of substance to your shit. You got to show your shit now. Let me see your skills. And I think that time is going to come back around soon. It might be a year or two years or whatever. But it's going to be a time when it's going to be like, "Okay, let me see where your skills is at." And you going to be judged on how you putting your words together. Whether it's an R & B song or a regular rap song.

I got entire notebooks with rhymes I never laid down or nothing. Because I always keep all my books. Because I be saying one day they going to be somewhere. I'm going to keep and leave it for my grandkids or whatever the case may be, and shit like that or whatever. Or it'll

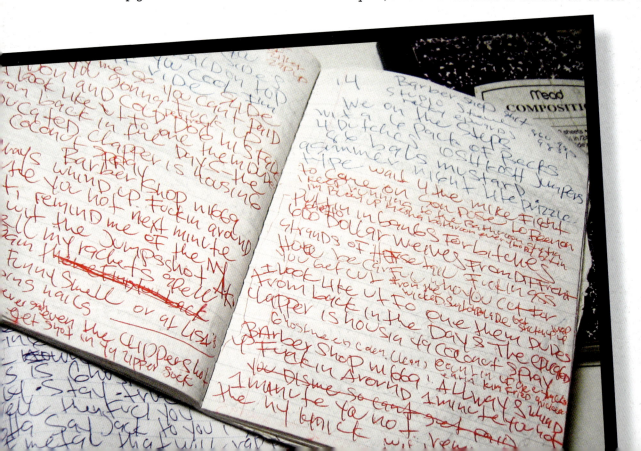

be in a fucking museum somewhere. Somewhere kids would like. Or the kids sell them for something, or whatever. I keep all my books with rhymes.

Shit, I still got books at my baby mother's house. That was years and years ago. And I lost books, too. I lost books when I had all my shit, and when I moved all my shit was in the studio. The man didn't pay the fucking rent, and they closed the studio down and took all my shit. Threw a lot of shit, all my old gear, everything away, mad Wallabees, mad shit I wore in videos, silk robes and shit.

> "But right now I might got like twenty books in my possession. And then probably got more, I know I got more scattered at my baby mother's crib and shit. Yeah. The one that's at my baby-mother crib, I might got another ten or twelve or so over there. It depends. It might even be more than that, I'm not sure."

And those notebooks are all crazy because sometimes I don't finish one rhyme on one page. Just say that I wrote the rhyme, but only eight bars of the rhyme was cool, because I want to scratch the rest of the other shit. But now I got to continue on another page. But that page might have words on it already, so I got to go to the bottom of that next, second page and write that rhyme. And now that goes with that. So I read from the top of the first one on the left-hand side, and then go to the right, all the way down at the bottom of the next page. And that'll be the other little bit of the four bars that was connected to there. And then it'll be some rhymes on the other. It'll be all over, so even if you trying to dissect my shit, it's like, "Where the fuck's this nigga going?" It's almost like a puzzle.

So some rhymes come out like that. Some rhymes I go all the way through. But yeah, I got verses in there that I even forgot the beat I was writing it to. Like, "Damn, what beat was that that made me go ahead and write that rhyme?" Or how did I say it? What was the flow on that? And I'll try to go ahead and relive it and get the flow. So I more than likely will catch the flow if I sit with it for maybe thirty minutes or something like that or whatever, like, "Okay, this is how I said it," for the most part, and shit like that. But I got books, though. I got books. I never went back to the books to pick out something that I'm doing because I always go with something new. But the books are still there, trying to figure out these rhymes and shit. I always say one day I'm going to go back in my books and get all those old raps, try to put them together and shit like that.

After we finished *Forever*, we hung around LA for a while. I was twenty-six, twenty-seven around that time and it was, like, we was just there. We wasn't there fronting or looking for trouble or doing all this other shit. We just was us. If you know us, you know we them brothers that's intelligent brothers that's hip to everything, and we can talk to you how you talk to us, and shit like that.

> "Of course, we were there when Biggie got shot. That was hard. In fact, when we'd come to the place where a nigga got shot or killed, you kinda felt like you just got shot yourself."

It was fucked up. I felt fucked up in my soul when they killed Biggie out there like that. I felt even worse because me and him had just gotten to shake that handshake at L.A. Live. At least I got to make some kind of peace with him, squash whatever beef might have been between us. And I didn't even really get to tell him what I wanted to tell him, like, "Yo, let's make some music," and shit like that. I felt fucked up when that was happening like that.

But I remember the girls coming in that same night when we lived in Oakwood. Because Oakwood is like little buildings and shit like that with apartments. So everybody had a sis. I forgot who I was with, who was staying in my apartment over there, I don't remember. But they came to the apartment early the next morning, five or six in the morning. I think they was drunk. Yeah, they came that same night and was like, "Yo, y'all was right there. Them Muslim guys was looking funny, I'm telling you. They was looking funny."

Because they tried to say a Muslim dude dressed in a bow tie and all the other shit had killed Big. But even before they had the sketch of the dude, one of the girls, she was up there, drunk and shit, her and her two homegirls or whatever, saying like, "Yo, I seen him, he was looking funny. They was even looking like sturdy Muslims," and shit like that.

So I'm like, "I really don't know what the fuck she talking about." Because I didn't know there was a Muslim they tried to blame it on. There was guys that was dressed like they was FOI (Fruit of Islam) or whatever and putting their work on. So I didn't even know that.

But she came in with her friends to our place. I guess she lived in the same building at that time. And was like, "Yo!" All loud and shit. You know how females be when they step in the club. They were regular girls. I mean, they wasn't really looking like they knew it was fucked up, but they were just more laughing at the fucking dude that's looking like a fake Muslim, they said. They was laughing at that. When you look at a real FOI brother, they come more sturdy. They're sturdy. They're moving in a militant way and this and that and the third. But they said this one right here was like, he didn't have that sense. Like, he wasn't built like that. So they're laughing at that.

So this was before it even came on the news. They came back to the house. I'm like, "Oh, shit. Where . . ." And I felt crazy fucked up. I felt, for a minute, while I was out there like that, because it's like, maybe because me and Big are from the same place, and as far as New York goes, and his music is "yo, yo." You know. Shit, he had fly music. Bitches loved it. "One More Chance" or whatever. That's the shit. That's like my favorite joint. So it hurt. It hurt me.

The whole thing was crazy. Shit was crazy, but I was crazy like . . . I don't know . . . because we just lost Tupac before that. So now we're losing this dude right here. So it was like, "Oh shit, yo, what the fuck?" Yeah. Shit was just . . . it was just the changing, man. It was the change. After that era? Things kind of changed. It changed the dynamics of where we at right now, because some of these rappers might not even be in place if both of those rappers was still here.

But I know everything is meant to happen for a reason. So I'm a firm believer in that. I just take it as how you take it, because God don't make mistakes. We do. People do. What's destined for us is . . . okay, we all got an expiration date, but you never know. Like, it just so happened that six months later, he'd go back to the essence right after Tupac go. It was like, what the fuck? I didn't even know that the cards lined up like that.

And Biggie was going out there with good intentions, though, from what I seen. I'm going back to California . . . he was going out there. He wasn't arrogant. It definitely was like when you got problems with somebody, you don't got problems with the whole fucking city. If I got a problem with a brother in Seattle, that's just me and that nigga in Seattle. I don't got a problem with all of Seattle. So I look at it like that. When he was coming, he was coming to do his little radio work, put his little work in. And do what he do and break out. Shit, I've never heard him kick dirt on Tupac or the West Coast like that.

No, he just went out there to promote his single. And it might've been at the wrong time. I don't know. Only God knows, but I don't know what he felt on his heart, because if he felt free on his heart to go ahead and do it, then, yo, you know what? But at the same time, he's twenty-five, twenty-six. So when you're young, you're still making stupid decisions. You don't know. I was still out there doing dumb shit at twenty-five and twenty-six myself. And if you would have told me that at the time, I would have thought I was making the right choices and shit. Now that I'm older, I say, "Damn, why the fuck did I do that at twenty-five and twenty-six?" I shouldn't have even did all that shit.

Yeah, we was doing shit. We was partying, bugging all the time, partying in the house. I remember one time me and U-God went to Brett Ratner's crib, and we wildin' out over there. I was mad drunk. I drank a bottle of fucking Seagram's gin damn near to the head, and I started pissing on his grass, pulling his fucking grass up. Everybody was looking at me . . . and I don't know, you got to go to U-God for that story. He was like, "Yo, I wigged out," but I remember wigging out, though. Just going crazy. Yeah, he was telling me, "Relax. Yo, you can stay at my house." But everybody looking at me: Heavy D, Leonardo DiCaprio . . . and I just wigged out.

I remember Brett Ratner. He was the one who did the million-dollar video for "Triumph" for us. So he started trying stuff. So I'm at his crib, yo, and to this day, I still say sorry, though. Wherever I see him, "Yo, yo, pardon me that time, B. Yo, yo, I'm sorry." Like, yo, I was just sitting there . . . I was drunk, man. I was drunk, just wilding. Pissed all over his fucking lawn. That's some shit Ol' Dirty Bastard would've did, but, yo, I don't know why I wigged out. I know I was drunk, but come on now. I ain't never wigged out like that before. I wasn't doing no other shit like that. No coke. No dust, or other shit like that. Hell no. It was just straight Seagram's gin. I remember, I drunk that shit. Think I might have had one of them long, skinny ones, but it was kind of short like a pint or something like that, or the cup size above a pint or whatever. And that shit was . . . yeah, B. Right to the fucking head. No chaser behind it or nothing, just out the bottle. Just trying to get right going over there. By the time I got there? Oh, man. It was a rizzy.

I don't know if it was a full moon . . . I don't know what the fuck it might've been . . . but yeah. Whatever it was, it was heavy. I was lit, and I was embarrassed. Lit and embarrassed because when U-God explained to me what I did the next day, I mean, when he telling me what I did that night, the next day. I'm like, "Yeah, I feel like a piece of shit." In front of all those niggas. Yeah. I'm over here, I'm in front of your face, pissing on the motherfucking plants or whatever. It was bad.

From my perspective, *Wu-Tang Forever* was just another album. We knew, okay, what type of promotion was going to go into it? But now we can get ahead to do at least 600K, 700K the first week or something like that. And I think, I don't know whoever dropped around the same time, I don't know if it was Biggie's *Life After Death* or something like that. But, yeah, we were looking to do our numbers, and we came out good with the double album.

But, to tell you the truth, it was just another day at the office. It was, "Ah, yo, you know what? Y'all got to get the video." We worked at it just like how we worked the first one. So we knew what it was. "Okay. You got these interviews you got to do, you got these photo shoots you got to do, you got that. All right. You got to make appearances on these TV shows." Then go do that. It wasn't in my mind like, "Oh, shit, get ready to blow up and make this all, what you call it? Rich." No, because we felt we had that feeling already, we had that feeling with the first album and then with all the other albums, with Method Man, with Dirty. With me and Rae, we had that feeling when we did *Cuban Linx*. Even when I did *Ironman*, it was like, okay, boom, there goes *Ironman*. And now we're doing the Wu-Tang thing again. So you were just out there with your brothers, trying to get the best that you can get out of it and the studio. And that was it.

Rage Against the Machine/Wu-Tang tour poster

And Loud spent money on it. Now we had serious studio money behind us. When you're able to spend money like that, it's okay, you got to go here. You got to be there and do that and do that and do this. And we was out there following up, we was following up.

Unfortunately, we didn't get a chance to do the world tour to support the album. We was on tour with Rage Against the Machine in Europe, but the check just got screwed. We screwed that the fuck up. We fucked ourselves from doing that because we could have finished the tour, so mega record sales were gone, just by pulling out of that tour, and doing all that.

Then, when we got back to New York, we cursed out the radio stations and they kind of banned us from HOT 97. They wasn't playing our record anyway. They was taking Bad Boy Records over . . . to us, that was how it was looking on the outside, ya'll playing all of their shit and then it's, "Yo, we not even getting no spins with "Triumph." "Triumph" was hitting hard at that time, too, but it felt like certain forces were saying, "They're speaking the truth, so watch these niggas."

So we was debating whether to do it or not—half of us wanted to do it, the other half didn't, like, "Yo, they're not playing it like this anyway." That's why we made the decision. No, we wasn't going to fuck with it, we were gonna come back and do the show. RZA said we needed to do it so HOT 97 wouldn't completely cut us off. We wanted to go on last, but they put Bad Boy on before us. And I bugged out again. I did wig out, not thinking, and said, "Fuck HOT 97, fuck that nigga." It was me again. Talking that stupid shit. I said it on stage in front of their fucking faces.

And again, you got to grow into yourself. You got to grow into this. If you thought you meant it back then, but you might get older and realize, "Why the fuck did I say that shit?" Why did I do that?

RISE OF A KILLAH: Ghostface Killah

Ghostface on a bullet train in Japan

CHAPTER 10

SUPREME CLIENTELE

Scientific, my hand kissed it
Robotic let's think optimistic
You probably missed it, watch me dolly dick it
Scotty watty cop it to me, big microphone hippie
Hit Poughkeepsie crispy chicken verbs throw up a stone richie
Chop the O, sprinkle a lil' snow inside a Optimo
Swing the John McEnroe, rap rock'n'roll
Tidy Bowl, gung-ho pro, Starsky with the gumsole
Hit the rump slow, parole kids, live Rapunzel
But Ton' stizzy really high, the vivid laser eye guide
Jump in the Harley ride, Clarks I freak a lemon pie
I'm 'bout it, 'bout it, Lord forgive me, Ms. Sally shouted
Tracey got shot in the face, my house was overcrowded
You fake cats done heard it first
On how I shitted on your turf
At times, Cuban Link verse yo
Check out the rap Kingpin, summertime fine jewelry drippin'
Face in the box, I seen your ear twitchin'
As soon as I drove off, Cap' came to me with three sawed-offs
Give one to Rae', let's season they broth

Lightning rod fever heaters, Knock-Kneeder Sheeba for hiva
Diva got rocked from the receiver bleeder
Portfolio, lookin' fancy in the pantry
My man got bigger dimes son, your shit is scampi
Base that, throw what's in your mouth, don't waste that
See Ghost lampin' in the throne with King Tut hat
Straight off

Supreme Clientele

Accolades for Supreme Clientele

Publication	Country	Accolade	Year	Rank
Addicted to Noise	United States	Albums of the Year	2000	23
Alternative Press	United States	Albums of the Year	2000	14
The A.V. Club	United States	Top 50 Albums of the 2000s (decade)	2009	28
The Boombox	United States	Top 10 Albums of the 2000s (decade)	2009	3
CokeMachineGlow	United States	Top 100 Albums of the 2000s (decade)	2010	2
Complex	United States	The Top 100 Albums of the 2000s (decade)	2009	8
Delusions of Adequacy	United States	Top 100 Albums of the 2000s (decade)	2010	15
eMusic	United States	Top 100 Albums of the 2000s (decade)	2009	6
FACT	United States	Top 100 Albums of the 2000s (decade)	2009	83
Hip-Hop Connection	United Kingdom	The 100 Greatest Rap Albums 1995–2005	2005	2
HipHopDX	United States	Top 10 Albums of the 2000s (decade)	2009	*
NME	United Kingdom	Albums of the Year	2000	36
One Thirty BPM	United States	Top 100 Albums of the 2000s (decade)	2010	86
Pitchfork Media	United States	The 100 Best Albums of 2000-2004	2005	19
Pitchfork Media	United States	The 200 Best Albums of the 2000s (decade)	2009	11
Playground	Spain	The 200 Best Albums of the 2000s (decade)	2009	10
Porcys	Poland	Top 100 Albums of the 2000s (decade)	2010	65
Rhapsody	United States	Hip-Hop's Best Albums of the Decade[34]	2009	2
Rock de Lux	Spain	The 100 Best Albums of the 2000s (decade)	2009	24
Rolling Stone	United States	Top 25 Hip-Hop Albums Ever (by Chris Rock)[35]	2005	14
Rolling Stone	United States	Top 50 Albums of 2000[36]	2001	*
Rolling Stone	United States	The 500 Greatest Albums of All Time[37]	2020	403
Slant Magazine	United States	Top 250 Albums of the 2000s (decade)	2010	59
Spin	United States	Albums of the Year	2000	11
Spin	United States	The 50 Best Albums of 2000-2004	2005	8
Stylus Magazine	United States	Top 101-200 Albums of All time	2004	179
Stylus Magazine	United States	Top 100 Albums of the 2000s (decade)	2010	27
Treble	United States	Top 150 Albums of the 2000s (decade)	2010	82
Treble	United States	Top 110 Albums of the 2000s (decade)[38]	2009	*
URB	United States	Top 10 Rap Albums[39]	2002	10
Vibe	United States	Albums of the Year	2000	14
The Village Voice	United States			*
The Wire	United States	50 Records Of The Year[40]	2001	

After *Forever*, I started working with RZA on *Supreme Clientele* in '98. On this one, I just knew I had to do up to whatever my standards were, because I was still a little bit upset with the way I handled *Ironman*. I just wanted to make this one where it's like, okay, I got no regrets. Where I wouldn't feel upset, but I didn't have pressure off of the Wu-Tang Clan. It was like, we did *Forever*, and now I got to try to uphold the flag.

I just did me. I just wanted to go pick out the right beats. Get the right beats, get the right people that belonged on tracks, the right skits and the right order, and let it go. I didn't want to rush it. There was still a deadline, but it really didn't feel rushed because what I like to do, I like to get the vibe of the album. So I would go to beats, get beats that I think are in my realm. Like that sounds phat to me. If it sounds phat to me, I like to go with that. I took that and even the skits and all that stuff like that. Even the people that I had on it, I felt that the instruments should be laid on the vocal track that they're on, and really that's it.

A lot of these albums, how they come out, be the frame of mind that you're in at that time. It's like, oh, shit, that's where your frame of mind was at. That's how it was. And if you're having fun and you're going to the studio you just having fun during the day, whatever is your fun, I don't care what it is. Girls, could be drugs, and that's your mood. That was it.

Like I said earlier, I made the right choice of beats and that was it. Because I like to work in the mornings. I like to get to work like ten, eleven in the morning and leave out of there by a certain time at night, but I was doing like a lot of all-nighters, just sleeping in there and shit like that, waking up and just doing shit, which was fine because we owned the studio anyway. Trying to make it to where it needs to be. It'd be times, other people might come in there and work, but I'm still there, though. It was people in the studio at all times. But in the beginning working on that shit, it was like, yeah, we was just in there. It was mainly the spirit that was over me at that time. That's what formed, molded *Supreme* like that. It was in my spirit. Like, alright, cool. But I knew I had to hurry up, had a time limit on that record, and had to get it done. This time it was like, I'm working through the summertime, I'm getting beats.

Around that time was when RZA had a flood in his apartment. He lost all the fly shit. I don't know why God did that, but it happens. But with those beats he had then, if he had managed to keep them? The game would have been looking real different. That run probably would have lasted five more years with all the shit he had in there. How many albums we would have been putting out? He lost so much dope shit. I mean, dope shit.

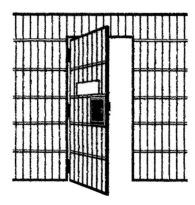

Then, in the middle of all of that, while I'm trying to work and get beats and shit, I fuck around and go to jail for six months from the Palladium nightclub shit.

Here's how that all went down. The Wu was touring and all that, and records had to get made, and so I just kept doing what I do, and kept my problems mostly to myself. Like, you don't go out there telling your problems to people. You know, you smile when you don't want to smile. So it was like a three-ring circus. It's like that song by Blue Magic called "Three Ring Circus," when it's like, this guy was a clown, making people laugh and all this other shit. But then when he got done and came home, he was just a lonely baker. But a lot of things don't make you happy. And plus, when you dealing with a lot of certain other shit, and you going through shit, it can start getting to you. And that's why motherfuckas turn to drugs or start drinking and doing all this other shit.

Now me, I ain't really do a bunch of drugs where I'm strung out and sniffing coke and all that other dumb shit. I probably had a couple of sips, drinking and shit. I think I might have probably blew a couple of bags of dust, or something like that, like in the 2000s or whatever. When I was doing *Supreme* and shit. Matter of fact, I know I did. That shit was around, and you started to fuck around and, "Yo, let me hit that." Now it's like, yo, it's back in your life now.

But that was it. After a while, I cut that down. Like right after that. And I don't even know why I went back to it. But, you know, because when me and Un was smoking, that shit was back like ages and shit like that. Probably, I might a did it in the '90s and shit like that. So that was like '98, '99. Because I remember I got caught with it. Like I went uptown one day, right, on like, I think by 116th or somewhere around there. And I bumped into, God bless the dead, Big L. I bumped into Big L, the rapper. He was real great. He from uptown, used be down with Cam'ron and all that, and rhyming with Jay-Z and all that shit.

But before I went to jail, that same night, when I left him because he was selling dust up there. And he had it fresh. So I said, "Yo, I need like four bundles." So he went and got me four bundles. And he got the shit, came down, came back with the money and shit. And like, "Yo, all right, yo . . ." kicked it a little. You know, "All right, yo, chill. You good? You good?" "Yeah, yeah, yeah. I'm good." I was out. I was out. Boom, jumped in the car. So we like three cars deep. So they pull the first two cars over, or whatever. But we was the stupid motherfuckas. We stood there and waited for them to do what they had to do with the other cars.

And the dumbass dude that was driving the car I was in, he going to go tell the cops like . . . because the cops was like started questioning us. Like, "Yo, what's up? What's y'all doing in this . . ." And I had a gun on me and I had a vest. So I had the gun in the whip, behind the dashboard, somewhere tucked in the glove compartment. And me and Bohn is in the car, and my cousin, and the other little dude is in the car and shit. So the little dude, he's driving and shit, he's like, "Yo, my uncle's Internal Affairs." Like that was going to scare the cops.

That motherfuckers was like, "Matter fact, get the fuck out the car." So remember, I got a vest on. They search me, I got the vest on. They like, "Yo, he got a vest" and this and that. So they getting to search the whole fucking car. They find the gun in the back of there and shit. They took all of us down. And they locked us up . . . but they had to let me go.

"But then the dude dry-snitched on me, and told them it was my gun, the one you let go. Dry-snitching means you're a rat. You didn't snitch in front of my face, you snitched behind my back and all that other shit. Like, you doing it without you thinking nobody knew. Because when the cops asked, 'So, yo, so who's gun was it?' or whatever the case may be, he went and told the police it was my shit."

So the cops gave me back the vest, but they followed the car all the way, going to Brooklyn. Remember, this was in Manhattan. So we took off. So I was in the car with RZA and them, and I got the dust on me still. They didn't find it. I had the dust stuffed in the sleeve of my goose. Like, I cut a little hole and just stuffed it in there.

So they smelled it. Like, "Where's the shit coming from?" They smelled the mint leaves and shit. But they couldn't tell. So I'm in the car with RZA and them, the car they pulled over. Then I'm looking at these niggas follow us. Like they was in like thirteen cars following us. And I'm like, "Yo, the fuck these niggas still coming for?" Every time we turned, they turned. But they trying to keep they distance. But I'm one of them quarterbacks. I see everything. I'm an all-seeing eye. Soon as you think I don't see it, I peep it. If you scheming or whatever, whatever. You know what I mean? I peep everything.

> "So I'm like, 'Yo, fuck this shit.' I said, 'Yo,' I said, 'roll up.' I'm rolling up right now. Like, you know what I mean? So I took one of the bags out, I rolled it up in the joint. I lit that shit and it just got me more amped up. It got me more like, 'Yo, fuck these cops.' So when we riding through Brooklyn, I said, 'Yo, pull over. Just pull over.'"

So as soon as we pulled over, I jumped out the car and I had the vest on still. And I just, as soon as I jumped out the car all I heard was, "Freeze! Get the fuck on the ground! Get the fuck on the ground!" It was like thirteen fucking cops on my ass, and it was scary too when you look at it. But it wasn't scary to me that day. When I look at it now, because they was all dressed in black. All in black, like you what I mean, like the black police coats. Because it was like kind of cold over there, it was like wintertime. So they had the police coats. Like just imagine like eighteen cops, in just all police jackets, all like that, at nighttime with guns pulled on you. With guns pulled on you. I wasn't listening at first. It's like, if I would have did anything stupid they probably would have shot me.

I almost got out like I was going to ask them like, "Yo, why the fuck is you following us?" So it's like by the time I stopped and opened up, they might have saw the door and everybody might have just ran out when they saw the door open. Or, stop or whatever. And I just heard "Freeze." You know, all that shit like that. And I had got locked up for that shit right there.

But then when I got locked up, I seen my friends and everybody back in the bullpen. You know, back where we was at. They took me back to Manhattan. And my man Bohn is telling me like, "Yo, this nigga dry-snitched."

So anyway, we all locked up still and we in there, going to court and all that. So I'm about to bail me and Bohn out, like, we got to get the fuck out of here. And I got the nigga that dry-snitched, he crying. "Ugh, God, don't leave me here, God. Please God, don't leave me in here. Get me out, God. Please, please, God. Please get me out, please."

I'm like, "Nigga, you in jail. There ain't supposed to be crying in jail. The fuck is wrong with you? What you crying in jail for? You in jail, nigga. You don't see these niggas in here, looking at, 'ugh God, please God, please. Please, please, please God, please.'" Man I left that nigga dead up in there. Fuck out of here. You going to fuck around and dry-snitch on me, you going to tell the police—come on, man.

They try to charge me with the gun. They gave me the six months, five years' probation, and all this other shit. I mean, I had to because I had the other case open. Remember, me and Un had the other attempted-robbery case open.

I thought about music while I was in jail, but I didn't really write nothing. When you in jail, you can't see nothing. All you can see is just inside the jail and all that other shit. Even if you go to the yard, I'm not seeing like nothing that's opening my mind, that's inspiring to me. I could look at a tree or a bird and become inspired by that and whatever's going on in your life at that time. I didn't write shit in there.

When I came back, because I worked on it before I went inside, I came back home and started recording in Florida, some of them tracks in the Hit Factory in Florida, going back to the city and it was different and shit.

I knew the name already: *Supreme Clientele*. I had joints. I came home and just wanted to finish that shit because I knew what I had already. So when I came home, that's what I did. I didn't let none of that other shit just stop me. Yo, man, I love hip hop at that time, too. I love hip hop. I want to show niggas, yo, who the real fucking Tony Starks, Ghostface. This is me in the flesh, ain't none of y'all could fuck with me. And this is what I came to do.

> "I started spreading my wings on *Supreme*. RZA was doing mad shit at the time, doing *Bobby Digital* at the same time and recording other motherfuckers' shit. He don't got time to sit down with you and to do it. You just grow, like a bird, just grow your wings and you flying, start flapping, motherfucker."

Like getting beats, whoever made the beat and it was up my alley, like shit that I like, then I'm going to take that. I'm going to ask for it. But if they send it to me, more likely it's for me specifically. And sometimes you could just have something, even if the track is just there, it's really like a loop. But it might be phat, that loop, and you don't really need nothing more on it. I rhyme to that.

Now a lot of producers really make the track for you. Like RZA is a producer, I'm not. I'm not a producer, I don't make beats. But what you are saying, overall, like going and mixing and this and that and the third. It's a job. You got to go to master it, you got to put the album together.

So when I did that shit, I made sure every track was crazy. It wasn't like *Cuban Linx*, because *Cuban Linx* was harder. Mine is just a little bit more well-rounded on different aspects. Like

Rae's straight to the point, like straight-up mafioso shit. This shit is dope in a different way. So I just wanted to show these motherfuckers like, "Yo, this is me. This is me. This is my mind. When you see my albums, you looking at my mind."

It was also the order of the music. Like I've said before, sequencing is important. This record is like a twelve-round fight. If you think it stumbles in the seventh, it'll come out in the ninth round swingin'. I changed this album around like twelve fucking times, just to get the mood right.

> "*Supreme Clientele* was a good piece of work. Had the right beat, I had the right vibe going with it. And my beat selection was like one of the best selections, and that was it. And the little Tony Starks gets into the shit, and it came out and it did what it did."

But timing is everything. *Supreme* came out at the right time. I finished it by the right time for it to come out at the right time. The people had that feeling when they heard it come out in February going on springtime. It's like, oh shit, because things are changing anyway when springtime comes. The people they just gravitated to it like that.

So I'm going back and forth from the case to the other and shit. And then they just on our ass. Like they just was following us all the time.

I remember one time, like the police, they were just so much on our backs, as far as being Wu-Tang and shit. The police was like following us so much. I caught them one day, in Manhattan. I don't know where they started following us from. But I just seen one car, just keep following us. And I see a light, and it just like, boof, boof. Like taking pictures. So I'm like, "Yo, I think these motherfuckas are taking pictures." So we see lights go off, boof. I'm like, "Oh, these motherfuckas." So I call my lawyer. I'm like, "Yo, I'm coming over, man. I got these motherfucking cops up my ass, right here."

They just follow every block we turn, they turn, and we doing this, they doing that. So they just wanted us bad. So I'm like, "All right, yo, I'm a come over there." So they taking they pictures. So we stopped. My lawyer was down there, near the courthouse, I think on Centre Street. He was on Lafayette. Lafayette's across the street from Centre. So I go upstairs in the building, me and my mans with us, we go upstairs in the building. And I'm trying to, like, telling my lawyer like, "Yo, these motherfuckas man, they following us." They didn't even know that I'm going in my lawyer's building.

They just probably taking pictures of us walking in and whatever. So I fuck around and, oh yeah, I told my lawyer, "We fucked around." And he went downstairs and approached the car. Like, "Why you following my client around?" They told him like, "Yo, get the fuck away from my car." They barked at him, and shit like that. So he came upstairs, telling me like, "Yo, these cocksuckers over here, like they think they the shit. They done told me to get the fuck away from the car." And all this other shit, and they got mad. And I think drove off. Because, you know, when you got a lawyer with you, you can't really do too much. Because them niggas know the law. They didn't even know I seen him. But then when my lawyer told them that shit, they probably was like, "This motherfucker. This motherfucker watching all this shit. He watched us from all the way."

They was trying to act like we was a fucking gang, and it's like the hip hop police and everybody. Everybody wants to just do they shit. Like trying to just peep out to see what the fuck you doing. So you know what, man? I ain't doing nothing right now. I'm cooling. Leave me the fuck alone. You're just to trying to live your life, do your own thing. And we chilling. Like, yo, at that time, we chilling and shit. I ain't selling no drugs, no tooling around, none of that.

Supreme Clientele

CHAPTER 11

DEF JAM . . . RUN

Psst
Yo (Yo), yo-yo (Yo), yo (Five-O)
Oh shit, yo (Yo, let me out), run

Aiyo, I jumped from the 8th floor step, hit the ground
The pound fell, cops is coming
Runnin' through the pissy stairwells, I ain't hear nothin'
Buggin', only thing I remember was the bullshit summons
So I stopped at the 2nd floor, ran across, cracks is fallin'
My pockets is lean, clean when I vanished off
Took off, made track look easy
The walkie talkies them D-T's had, black, they was rated P.G.
Run, I will knock your bug, no, quick flag the car down
Take me to . . . Yo yo yo, Ghost here they come now!
Errr! Pull off quick, back up, hit the bitch, dog
Turned down Hill, light the Marley spliff
Run! I will not get bagged on the rock
Run! I seen what happened to Un, they bad with they cops
Run! They amp shit, plan shit, destroy evidence
Fuck a case, I'm not comin' home with no fifty six

Die with the heart of Scarface and take fifty licks
Before I let these crackers throw me in shit
Bounce if you a good kid, bounce, do the bird hop
Curse, swerve to get served, these cocksuckers got nerve
Heard I was killin' shit, they must got word
That I told the chief of Rich Port I don't wanna merge

Run! If you sell drugs in the school zone
Run! If you gettin' chased with no shoes on
Run! Fuck that! Run! Cops got, guns!
They givin' out life like bird tons
Run! If you ain't do shit, you it
That next felony, nigga, it's life, three zip
So, run! Hop fences, jump over benches!
When you see me comin' get the fuck out the entrance!
Run! Fuck that! Run! Cops got guns! Muthafucka . . .

Supreme Clientele was my last Sony album. Razor Sharp Records had separated from Sony/Epic. So when they separated, I left too. RZA was doing a lot of his business. He had shit everywhere. But as far as Razor Sharp, we parted ways. I got off the label and became a free agent. And I went over to Def Jam. Lyor Cohen, the president of Def Jam, opened the door for me. So me and Lyor was just getting started, but then he messed around and got another job. When he left, my album, *The Pretty Toney Album*, was already on the market. After he left, everything just went downhill. Even the building changed. They were changing it to some R & B shit. And you got to be somewhere people believe in you. If nobody's believing in you, you're going to just be sitting there.

For *Pretty Toney*, I just did it. I just went to Miami and did it. It was just go out there, record some tracks, and do that. And that was it. When *Pretty Toney* came out, that's when I stopped smoking weed because it was getting too much on me. It was like, I'd smoke weed, I'd smoke it getting up, trying to write some rhymes, and I kept forgetting every line I wanted to write. And then I wasted a bunch of money in the studio because I got three o'clock studio time and I'm not getting there until like ten, eleven o'clock at night. And then when I get there, I'm not trusting my judgment on when I'm in there trying to spit. I'm in the booth and I'm questioning myself, like asking my man, Joe, "Is that it?" And I only will be there for like two hours or three hours. And then I'll just leave again. But I had $2,500-a-day block of studio time. And I'm in the penthouse, right? They pay for the penthouse. And I got another apartment that's inside the same building for my mans.

It was too much money. It took me eighteen months to finish one fucking album. And that's when I said, "You know what? I'm not doing this no more." And I stopped smoking weed ever since. I can't focus like that. It's not for me no more. It just attacked a certain part of my brain, made me fucked up and made me feel real light in the ass. First of all, weed makes you lazy. It made me lazy. It just wasn't for me no more. My brain, I guess, started rejecting that after a while.

And it did that in the middle of the *Pretty Toney* shit. So I had to make a decision to leave that shit. Like, "Man, you wasting too much money." Def Jam's mad at me. Motherfuckers probably don't want to work with me no more and shit. They were like, "We spent all this money on you," and they going to come down and check to see what I'm doing? And they really didn't get nothing when they came down. I should have tracks done, and I didn't have shit done. I was fucked up. That's why I had to stop smoking. My decision-making wasn't on point. And all those songs is fucked up.

If I had to do it again, I wouldn't have picked those beats. I wouldn't have picked some of those pieces. I would have been a more dangerous writer. So I just tried the best I could just to get the album out. And it's cool, but it ain't. It wasn't my vision. It was my vision while I was fucked up in the head, trying to figure out what beats should I use. I use this beat and this and that and that. But now I'm behind the clock, and I got deadlines. The label needed their music. And I had "Tush" with Missy Elliott on the track. Because at that time, Missy was hot. She was doing her thing. And I love Missy. She's fucking dope. She's one of the best. Motherfuckers can't even fuck with her to this day. Her mind is different. I like people that do different shit, like Andre 3000, Missy Elliott, the people's minds that's like, they're here, but they're not here. That's why Kanye is a fucking genius, too. And Missy's one of them artists like that. So I'm like, "Yo, you know what? All right, let me do this shit called 'Tush.'" I already was working on it, but I had her in mind.

And I'm like, "Yo, let me see if I can get a little dance track." And it might be, getting it to just be like, "Yo, you know what, take me in another fucking stratosphere and fuck around radio." Radio didn't even play that record because it kept saying to tush all day. Tush, tush, tush. And these niggas . . . these motherfuckers, they bleeping it and saying like this and that and the third. And "Push" didn't even stand for what we think it is—that was some nasty shit. It was like, "Push, I want to get up in that tush." The tush was the nasty word of anything at the time. But if I was to say "tush" as a hook right now, they'd play that shit 24/7. Missy killed it, but it just ain't work for me. And I had to go back to the drawing board.

Even the R & B album (*Ghostdini: Wizard of Poetry*) I did on Def Jam—to me, that's one of my best ones besides *Supreme*, and *Bulletproof Wallets* was dope, too. I just couldn't get a couple of samples cleared on it. I couldn't find the sample for the joint, there with Slick Rick. If I would've had those three up there, it would've been a classic, like *Supreme*.

When *Pretty Toney* came out, we also did a book, *The World According to Pretty Toney*, and a few skits for MTV. You just seeing the world through my eyes or what I think about shit. It wasn't nothing deep. It was nothing that was just about real shit. *Pretty Toney* on money. *Pretty Toney* on love. *Pretty Toney* on livin', that sort of thing. I don't know if they seen something or whatever the case may be and wanted to do that, or they might've just had this shit and just wanted me. It was a book, and they had a couple of skits on MTV. They shot a few episodes. Wasn't really big, heavy like that. After the episodes were released, they wanted an audiobook, too.

RISE OF A KILLAH: Ghostface Killah

About this time is also when "Summertime" by Beyoncé came out. And how that song came about was one of my men had her vocals. I was in Miami, trying to write the *Pretty Toney* album. He's like, "Yo, I got a Beyoncé song. I got a Beyoncé song. It's a dope one. Yo, you should get on this one. It's dope."

I said, "All right, bring it over."

He bought it over and played it. I was like, "Yo, this shit fire." I broke it down, took the beat, and just wrote that shit. Laid it down, sent it back home. I think I might've sent it to Kay Slay first. It grew legs automatically. Before I know it, they're playing that shit. I wasn't even hearing them, because they wasn't playing it like that. They weren't even playing it at all in Miami. I'm hearing it in New York, that shit's spinning every fucking time, but I didn't even know it. I didn't even catch that wave. I didn't know what it was. I just know I did it, and sent it out and that was it. And I think that's why Jay-Z called me for the concert at Madison Square Garden. Because he could have put Sean Paul on it. To go do the other song he got, but he chose me. So I'm like, "All right, cool." And I just ran with that.

Ghostface and Slick Rick backstage at Jay-Z and Beyoncé's farewell concert, Madison Square Garden

Beyoncé and Jay-Z's farewell concert at Madison Square Garden in 2003. That shit was crazy. I did the sound check with Beyoncé earlier that day. And I'm like, "Yo, what you want me to do?"

She kept it gangster. And that's what I liked. She said, "No, just do you." Just like that. And I looked at her like, "Word?" "Yep." And that was it. We sung through it like one time, maybe two. One or two times, that was it. It was over. I had to go to the hotel, get changed, and then come back. By the time I came back, and had the robe and all that shit on, because she didn't know that the change was coming, it was like, when she seen me on stage, it was different. It was like, "Oh shit, where the fuck did this nigga come from?"

Beyoncé and Ghostface, Madison Square Garden

On the side, first it started okay. Slick Rick came in the back. He came, because I reached out to him, "Yo, yo, let me hold your chains," I asked him. "If I could just do this thing out here tonight. Just come through." But he came and surprised the niggas. He didn't tell me he was coming. I asked him like a week before it or whatever. He didn't even tell me. He just came with a bang and got me. That's how God worked, yo, because I could've went on stage, and he might've missed me. But he came. He came at the right time, right before we were starting to go on. I don't know how the fuck that happened. And he just, I'm like, "Yo." I had my pieces on or whatever, but he just came and he just drowned me in his shit. So he like, "One, two, three, four," going across the neck. Oh shit, yeah. Now my powers is really coming. My Iron Man powers is coming out now.

To hear the crowd, it was like, all I heard when I stepped on the stage was that big crowd. I can't do the sound. Like, "Oh, shit," and I just got lost. It was a moment to step on stage with her, and the crowds is in the uproar. But I almost forgot my lead-in, because I'm asking Mike, when I got to the steps, because she was on stage. I'm like, "Yo, what the fuck is my lines?

I forgot how I come on. How I come on?" And he's like, "I don't know. I don't." I'm like, "He ain't no fucking help," but the song, my part getting ready to come on. The power of God just came over me. Yo, God just smacked me in the back of my head and just . . . And the first line came out, yo. But it came out while I was walking on stage. I didn't even know my bars going up the steps.

That's what I said, God kicked me in my ass, or he just smacked the shit out of me in the back of my head or something. Just sit back, and it just came out. And the crowd just went like that, just went crazy like that. And, yo, it was in my bones. That's why I was just like, "Yo, I appreciate Hov for giving me that moment, because he could have not even called for me. He could have just been like, "Yo, you know what? No." You know me, but that was a big look for me. It was a big look for me at that time right there, too. And it was a nice song. So I got a chance to share the stage with the queen.

Bulletproof wallets—it's almost like slang, like it could have been a saying or something like, "yo, bulletproof wallet, my wallet is bulletproof." Yeah. It just came to me one day standing in the living room and I just said it, "Yo, Bulletproof wallets" and I'm like, yeah, that's it, I like that—bullets, bulletproof. Like your wallet is bulletproof—niggas can't get in your wallet.

Regarding the artists on my albums, some people might've been in the studio and stuff like that at the time or whatever, like the Killa Sin. I don't know if RZA had put him on like that or whatever. I forgot, but first off you got to sound like you could fit on it. And Killa Sin murdered it, he murdered it. Sway murdered it. Superb was murdering it. You got to just feel it. My man Banks, Bankie, God bless the dead, too. We made it, it's like these guys fit the track. So you got to find them, if I choose an artist, I'm going to be like, "Yo, you know what Jadakiss or yo, Nas, or Sheek Louch should do it."

But you got to know your instrument, cause everybody's voice is their instrument. Like, nobody sounds like Nas. So you got to think of it like, oh shit, yo, this voice was on top of this.

That's how I looked at it. And it was like, oh shit, you know what, let me see if they want to fuck around or whoever want to get on a track. And that's it—you just put it together.

Bulletproof Wallets was the regular process. They just told me to do those kinds of records like that. But you know what? It got slept on, because RZA lost the sample to the song I had with Slick Rick. He couldn't find it. He couldn't find where he got that from. And then, who else? Barry White denied me for "The Watch," right? You know how "The Watch" come on? Tony for mayor, all that shit? That shit is chunky. And then a song on there called "Flowers," the original beat for it was murdered.

And then if I would have had "The Sun," because the song with Slick Rick was called "The Sun." So if I would have had "The Sun" on it like that, yo, now we getting some. It's like, oh my God, those is two fucking fireballs out the gate. And then the sample that they had to scratch from "Flowers," it's like, no.

Those three things right there. Listen, I'm the most consistent nigga in rap. As far as coming out the gate. If I would have got those samples, had those on there like that and the original "Flowers" beat, because they wouldn't clear the sample. If I would've had that on it? Yo, this would have been almost like *Supreme*'s twin brother, something like that. This would have been right up there with *Supreme*, but only *Supreme* probably would have had a little bit more of more funny skits, because we had "Who Would You Fuck" skit, the "Crackheads" skit, and shit like that. But other than that, no, *Wallets* would have been right there.

In 2004 I did *718* as part of Theodore Unit. I'm the one that came up with the name. The original thing was supposed to be Thinkers and Doers. But when you take your homeboys from the street, nobody wants to do shit. So we could not live the name like that. So you got people, brothers around you who don't think of shit, they just want to get high all day. And if an idea did come, it don't get lived out, it don't get done. So you're not doing it.

"*718* was like a mixtape with a bunch of my guys. We just got a bunch of songs together, a couple of my guys, and we just did them and just sold it to Sure Shot Recordings. It was just a bunch of songs, this guy had this song, I had that song, I had that. Yeah, that was it. It wasn't like *Ironman* or *Supreme*—those are my albums. *718* was a mixtape."

Then me and Trife Da God put out *Put It on the Line* in 2005 under Starks Enterprises label, just trying to launch the label. Honestly, I don't even remember that album. At that time, my mind was just somewhere else, I just was doing shit just to do it, and that's it. Because I know it's not a piece of work. Like, even though everybody put it a couple of songs, and had done this, and brought this to the table, and brought that, it was like, it's a mixtape. It isn't an album, album to me. A mixtape is just something that you put together just easy. My albums, I got to really know that's the beat, I got to really know. I really take my time, when I'm in the zone, and really write, I write. With a mixtape, it's like, I'm not going to say the lines don't count, but it's just like, "Yo, give me my check." You just worried about the check, give me the shit. It's shit like that. It's like a compilation album. It's like this guy got a record, this guy got a record, this guy got a record. All right, get on this record right here. But I got so much other work to do, I'm not concentrating on writing a mega rhyme. A rhyme that you hear and go, "Oh, shit. He really came with his blade out." I don't give a fuck. On these, I'm throwing butter knives. Yeah. I'm throwing butter knives—I'm not throwing Ginsus around back then.

That's why it's Jack City Entertainment, right now, because "jack" means "to take," and we got to go and take this shit. So we got to take ours. If you was to get jacked out here for your shine, somebody jacked you for all your jewelry, they snatched it off your neck, they took it from you. So Jack City is like, "Yo, we got to get ahead and just jack everything." Gotta jack that shit, you heard.

Now *Fishscale*, that title came from dealing with cocaine. When you got the fish scale, you got the top-of-the-line coke. And when you turn the coke a certain way, you can see the scales in it. Like the same way you see the scales on a fish, you turn it a certain way in the light and it might get a little shiny. It goes from shiny to different colors. You tilt it . . . you got cocaine on a fish scale, you might tilt it this way, and it'd be like it's sparkly, but then it's not sparkly, sparkly, then it's not. And that's how fish is. It's called iridescent. Yeah. Where the light changes the color of it as you tilt it around. So when I named it, I just said, "Yo, you know what? This is top of the line shit right here. And, yo, this album is *Fishscale*." Because everybody wants the top-of-the-line coke.

> **"When I did *Fishscale*, I put too many songs on it. I put too much unnecessary shit on it I could have just left out. It was too much. When I could have just broke that down and been like, 'Yo, you know what? Give me this little ten-eleven song brick right here.' I didn't need all of it, but I was still in the process of learning. I'm still in the process of learning."**

I'm learning to skit, I'm learning how to do skits. I'm learning how to triple and double up my hooks and shit like that. All that stuff I learned, because I didn't know about really doubling and tripling to make it sound more heavier, in my early days. I mean, yes, *Supreme Clientele*, *Ironman*, and shit like that, I didn't know that, and now I know if you could do without a couple of songs, so what? But I thought, damn, I made a lot of songs and it might sound a bit rough, but I got to keep it. No, you ain't got to keep it.

Yeah, because when I got to *More Fish*, we just had to hurry up and do it. They wanted another album for December so they could make their quota, and do all this other shit like that. And that's how that came about like that. I really had no time. I had maybe six weeks to do that shit, or two months or something. The studio just needed it by that time. So I just said, these are just songs that was left over from *Fishscale*, that I could have put on there, either one. And that was it, a lot of leftover shit, so I said *More Fish*. That was it, simple shit.

That collaboration with Amy Winehouse, I just got the call. I think Mark Ronson got the beat or whatever, did the music. He called up and wanted me on it. Because I did a song for him. I've known him for years, ever since I did the "Ooh Wee," the record with Nate Dogg. So he called back, I think for me to get on that. But Def Jam fumbled the ball. I could of sold millions of that record right there. But they thought I was playing, they thought it wasn't going to be shit. They didn't pay attention to the shit.

I had Shawn Wigs, Cappadonna on here. Also, I had Kanye, he and Ne-Yo did the remix on "Back Like That."

Ghostdini: Wizard of Poetry in Emerald City: Since my records and shit wasn't really going nowhere. I said, "You know what? I'm going to make an album with all fucking singles." They really got to work my shit now. They still ain't work that shit. That's why I did it just in case y'all beefing like, "Yo, you don't give us the right records." I said, "I'm a R & B this album real quick."

I'm a wizard at poetry, and this is my shit, so when it come to getting descriptive and trying to write music, and being in that frame of mind, it's like, "Yo!" That's why when you hear songs like when I rhymed over "Holla," with the words, like, "La, la, la, la, la, la," you know what I mean, the Delfonics, when I rhymed over them? I love old beats more than I love the new, like old show records, they're better than regular records. And I love R & B. So that gave me a chance to get ahead and be like, "You know what? Def Jam can't front now, because I'm going to hit these with like fifteen singles."

I got John Legend, Estelle. I had Lloyd, Raheem DeVaughn. I got Fabulous up there with Shareefa on "Guest House." I had a bunch of motherfuckers on that record, and Def Jam still couldn't do this shit. That's when I knew it was over. Like, "You couldn't market the John Legend record, you couldn't put that out?" And this nigga's a fucking Grammy Award winner. And when I saw him, I felt embarrassed, because he said, "Yo, what happened? This song was dope." I'm like, "Yeah, I know, these niggas. It was Def Jam." It's like I didn't know what to say to him.

So it almost seemed like Def Jam wanted me out that fucking building anyway, in the midst of it, while it's crumbling, you know what I'm saying? And then the one dude that did say, "You know what? I'm going to help you out, son," was the dude on that . . . God rest his soul, he got killed. Suicide. Shakir was his name. He said, "Yo, man, I'm going to help you out." And, like, not more than like two or three months later, he died.

But John Legend got the Grammy. Yeah. They just didn't back it the way they should've backed the record. They didn't back it right, and it was like, "Yo, John Legend got the Grammys and L.A. Reid wanted Baby."

> "Out of all my albums, I liked that one the most, and I had the right singles up there, and Def Jam just didn't do what they had to do. It had me so frustrated. That's when I knew like, 'You know what? You dropped the ball, nigga. I gave you fifteen records. They was all singles. I'm done with this shit.' That was it. I think that was my last album up there. I'm not sure, but I was done."

RISE OF A KILLAH: Ghostface Killah

Nowadays, I'd go with an independent label over a major. These majors is robbing the shit outta you, keeping your fucking masters, they doing all this other sucker shit. Now maybe if you was on a major, and they rocked with you for like one year, just to get your name up, and then go indie, that's kinda cool. Maybe two years, or just do two albums, that kind of thing.

Apollo Kids: Def Jam was expecting a sequel to *Supreme Clientele*, but I gave them *Apollo Kids* instead. Why would I give them that (*Supreme II*), and you ain't even doing nothing for me? Because the shit was all over the place there. You got new people coming in doing this, doing that. It's too much. Jay-Z leaves, and then here go this guy. It's just too much. It was just too much. No disrespect.

36 Seasons: Yeah, we laid that down in about eleven days, give or take. That was quick.

The *Sour Soul* album with the Canadian jazz instrumental hip hop band, BadBadNotGood. I got the call from Mike. He's like, "Yo, they got these guys in Canada." My man Frank Dukes is from out there. I think it was him that came with it. He sent the beats over, and it was just crazy. It was crazy. That group right there ain't no joke. They dope. And Frank Dukes, he's a dope producer, too. He's just dope. It wasn't real experimental. I don't take shit that serious. I know what I can do, and I know what I can't do. I wasn't in the studio with them. Frank Dukes had made beats, and he sent them. I guess he took my vocal and put them over the beats. Not live where I'm in the studio with them, but they made it live and sent it over to me, so I was rapping over the live performance recording.

DOOMSTARKS with MF DOOM: I came out to SXSW and the *DOOMSTARKS* record was going to come out. And we did this crazy setup. Doom couldn't get into the country, so they had him on film rhyming and while I was live in person in front of the film. In Austin, Texas. South by Southwest. We did that shit in Texas, and there was fifteen hundred people going crazy. The fucking screen was gigantic. It was like fifty feet tall, we were in sync and did the whole album—it was crazy!

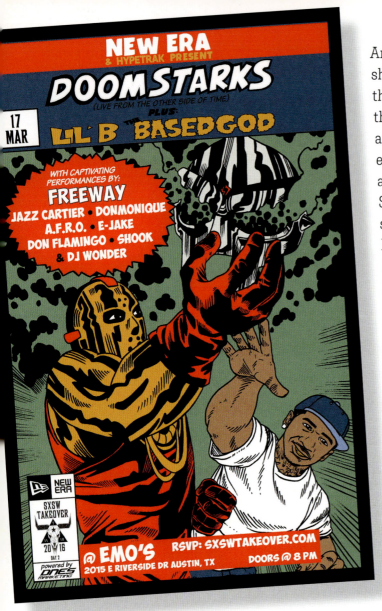

And the kids ate it up, they loved that shit. They just wanted to hear more of that *DOOMSTARKS*. They did. And that album posts a big finish. He got all the parts and everything. He had everything, but you know one thing about Doom, he took his time on things. So I don't know what he had up his sleeve. He laid all the beats. So I sent him all the rhymes and stuff like that, but he just take his time. I guess when he felt like something needed to go. Because everybody been screaming for him for years. So they asking me and I'm like, "Yo, no, it's on him. He got everything." So now when time is passing, I'm telling Devin, his director, like, "Yo, listen, let's finish that album. Let's get it done." But let me just go in and just . . . since the verses like mad years old, because it's been over maybe ten years or more. So I'm like, "yo, let me just do my verses, let me do the same verse, but let me just say it over, because when I was recording that I really didn't like the spot where I was recorded. Now there's better sound, let me redo my verses, let me record it over." And he agreed to it, but I don't know, it just never happened. And I talked to Devin after Doom's passing, he's like, "Yo, his wife got everything." Because we could still get it and put that out. I'm like, "Yo, we're going to have to. We're going to have to one day just do that."

CHAPTER 12

MONEY COMES FIRST

"We Made It"

"Tony Starks fights again for survival,
and by just a thin thread of electric current
wins another victory."

Uhh, c'mon, yeah, c'mon y'all
(Bounce wit us) Hip-hop
(What? Celebrities, what?)
(Street corner) For all my niggas
Crack spot niggas

Chicken ass mothafuckas, envious bitches
Yo, you know what y'all . . .

[Ghostface Killah]
Yo, spotted at a mirage, Ghostface swarmed by groupies
Mingle 'mong stars, I come in cat, invades Mars
Highlight of the century, first bet placed upon entry
Fainted when the book mentioned me
Keep ballin', new systems, high sciences
Drop that, Ghost listenin', track sizzlin'

Angelica, Judy Plum for bitches, Goines King of the century
Best sellers, but niggas stay together
Posted up trucks, leanin' on the Benz
Cinemax smile shot in thirty-five lens
You program, broke bottles of Dom
Seven inch bangles, back breakers
I'm a dope fiend, look at my arm, Popeye strength
Rap with a British accent, Gucci clothes
Dennis Coles in the latest fashion blow backs in
Flip raps like forty-eight bundles
Dinner plates, deadly front gates, celeb Bryant Gumbel

[Ghostface]
Uh-huh, uh-huh
That's right y'all
Street corners
Jail niggas
Riker's Island
Ge-Grey Haven
Big Un
That's right y'all
Word up
All y'all, all y'all crumbs
We made it, nigga
Step the fuck off
True indeed, true indeed
Yeah, Ready Red
That's right, my nigga Born
That's right yo
Lil' Free in the feds
That's right, you'll be home nigga
Yeah, we made it
Yeah, C Allah, word up
That's fam
Yeah, check it out
Staten Island
True indeed
Five boroughs
Check it, uh-huh

Money Comes First

Mike Caruso: To me—and this is my skewed opinion—but I don't think there's a more interesting character in the Wu-Tang Clan than Ghostface Killah. So you got a guy who's one of the best writing lyricists, probably, at the top ten, in the history of rap music, as far as a true writer and lyrical genius. Super underrated. You got a guy who's wearing bathrobes, with diamond-studded bathrobes. The first guy—I mean, Slick Rick came with the heavy chains and all that, remember? But all due respect to Slick Rick, Ghost wore them onstage, if you remember. That picture was taken during, I think, the Jay-Z concert, right? And he put Slick's jewelry on, and those thirty chains weighed about a pound. Ghost was the first guy to put five pounds of jewelry around his neck and another three pounds on his arm. So he had a million-dollar bird (Ghost designed the eagle bracelet and got it created by Jason of Beverly Hills.) The bird was put into storage with Jason for twenty or twenty-five years or so. Recently we melted the bird down and made a coin of solid gold with an NFT for it, and we're going to release that. A one-of-a-kind bird is now a coin with digital art. I have pictures of it, I got pictures of it melting, and I got pictures of the NFT. A million-dollar big disc chain on his neck, with the robes, talking all that real street shit.

See, people forget about this with Ghost. This is the guy who terrorized New York City. He and Dirty chased Biggie Smalls out of a club when he was having the beef with Dirty. It was a party at a club called Esso, and Ghost and Dirty walked in. And I was at the bar because I was working with the club at the time. Penny Flynn owned the club. We did a party for Ol' Dirty Bastard there that Ghost was booked to post with Dirty. Biggie came to the club at like ten AM when the door had just opened, and he bought about six bottles of Cristal, and he's sitting there with two chicks. And there were like maybe twenty people in the building. And he's drinking the champagne with them. And coming through the front door, you hear "Soooooooo" and all the Wu-Tang calls. Dirty just arrived. Biggie looked up and said, "It's time to go." Ran out the back door of the club, Ghost and Dirt saw him running out the back, ran back out the front, and the only thing we heard from inside was gunshots. I think it had to do with Biggie supposedly copying Nas's album cover, and then I think Raekwon commented on it and Ghost commented on it on *Only 4 Cuban Linx*... Something about the kid on the cover of the album, and then Biggie had some slick commentary about champagne and COOGI sweaters and Versace gear before everybody. And Ghost was big on Versace silks and drinking champagne out of the bottle at the time as well himself, but more on some wearing it on the block, not needing to go to clubs and all that with it on. But it was something in that vein where Dirty called them out, and then there was a beef between them.

Ghost also beat up Busta Rhymes and his crew backstage at the Palladium. It was him, Method Man, and I want to say Un maybe and those guys. And they got into a scuffle with the Flipmode Squad backstage, and Ghost basically unspooled the emergency fire hose and was swinging it with the big brass fire hose end. He was swinging it around and hitting people with the brass hose end.

He got shot in the neck. Both of his henchmen were in jail for life for murders. Now at the same time, you got this same guy who does records crying about his girlfriend cheating on him.

I first met Ghost during the early second part of his album, right after he came out of jail. It was early in his career, he was still recording *Supreme Clientele*. I've been with him for twenty-four years.

I was working on an album with Authorized F.A.M. Cappadonna's younger brother, Lounge, and my brother, Q, had a group. I was recording their album at Mystic Studio, and Cappadonna came in to do a feature on it. He featured on two or three songs and then we basically went on tour opening for Method Man, opening for Method Man and Redman for the *Doc's da Name* album tour.

Redman and Ghostface

So I do that tour and then I start going to the studio, meet Ghost in the studio, and he had a tour coming up to promote *Supreme Clientele*. Divine, RZA's brother, said "Hey, you just did that tour." He met me on the tour while he was out there with Method Man. He said "you were on the road with your group. You were very efficient, never missed a gig. Never late, blah, blah, blah. Why don't you tour manage Ghost?" So I went on as a tour manager for Ghost on the *Supreme Clientele* promo tour. That's how we became close while we were on the road. I gave him a really good insight into and education on the business the right way. He's like, "yeah, I want to hire you as my manager." He didn't really have anyone managing him before that. I took care of some of his understanding of touring earnings and showed how the costs were inaccurate and I shaped up the costs and the earnings for him to make more money. That's when he was like, "No, you need to work for me."

And it was more than just the financial aspects I worked on, too. Part of Ghost's thing was the kind of things that he wanted me to take care of for him. These are the couple things we got to focus on. One, was diabetes and making sure his sugar don't go down, making sure he always had orange juice, chocolate available if he needs it, making sure there's always food on tour buses when he needs it. The other thing was no pork and all the byproducts that we can't eat. And the third thing was making sure he never has guns around him, specifically him, because he had a two-strike felony with guns already.

This was around the time he had also just come back from Benin. I met him and he got sick with malaria, recovered from that and then he was still on probation for the gun and the vest. So when I came on board, I straightened all that out. We were writing him letters and getting Eric Wilson and Peter Schwarz to write him letters for touring. And I had to go meet with his probation officer and get him cleared to travel and all that. And we worked through all that, and we actually got him released from probation a year early because of his good record and his work ethic.

If we could do all this right, he said, "I'll never go back to jail again. I need to get to all these concerts on time and structure everything and do it right. And I don't want to have to worry about none of this stuff, and my diet and diabetes has got to be right." He started training at the gym nonstop to bring his sugar down, to rebuild muscle tissue, and I was calling up dieticians and all kinds of things for him. When we were on the road, we were in the gym every morning, working out before we'd leave or go anywhere.

So after that tour ended, he had great success with *Supreme*. We made every date on the promo tour, and three events happened. First, Polly Anthony (president of Epic Records) basically said, "Let's do another album."

Now at this time Ghost had an entire catalog of rock and rap groups. He had his own label deal at Sony. And at the time Razor Sharp was losing their deal at Sony for not delivering albums. They were behind on their delivery dates. And Ghost wanted to start his own label. Then Divine lost his company to Sony in the lawsuit. But Ghost took RZA's and Divine's side at the time, and wouldn't cooperate with Sony in court. They told him, "If you cooperate in court with our side of the arbitration, we'll sign the rock group, we'll sign the rap group you want to represent, we'll give you the imprint deal, and we're going to cut you a check for about five million."

> "But Ghost said, 'No, I won't go to court against RZA and Divine.' And they basically said, 'Either do it or you're out' And Ghost said, 'I'd rather be out than turn my back on my brothers.' They end up losing in court anyhow."

Second, Lyor Cohen calls me and says, "Hey Mike, I understand you're managing Ghost."

"Yes, I am."

"I want to bring the deal to Def Jam."

And Ghost and I negotiate his deal, leaving Sony to move to Def Jam. So Lyor gave us the curse in the gift, right? He gave us a five-year album deal. Five-year guarantee. And gave Ghost a really nice, sizable budget.

So now we're at Def Jam, and then we spent at least a year recording an album—which ended up being three albums—in Miami. Finally, Lyor actually came down while we were doing that first album. He sat me down, Ghost is recording, he said, "Michael, I got to talk to you."

I go, "what?"

He goes, "We had a talk about being broke, about the people you keep around you when I first brought you in."

I said, "Yeah."

He goes, "Get rid of all the broke people. Get them out of your lives. Keep rich people around you so you can get richer. You're never done with your business. Keep looking for new business opportunities, building on top of that." And started drilling in my head the importance of the branded partnerships and the liquor companies and everyone else that could offset expense.

And he goes, "Here you are a year into this album. You've spent over a million bucks. And I get it, you're living in Miami in a penthouse. You're having a good time. You're in the studio every night, everything's paid for on our budget. I hear you're playing twenty rounds of golf a month. But if you want to continue in this business, you'll get me a single in the next month and deliver me an album within sixty days. Or that five-album deal you have will end. And nobody else in the industry's going to give you a job."

So I call Chris Lighty at Violator; I knew him as a teenager. I say, "Yo, I need a sure-shot single. Who do you got? Could I get Missy?"

He said, "Sure. Gotcha, Mike." Sent her a beat, she came back with the "Tush" record, and we had a single. I wrapped up a mixed Ghost album in the next forty days, and the rest is history.

A big piece of why *The Pretty Toney Album turned* out the way it did is because Def Jam wanted a radio record, Lyor and them wanted something a little more sexy, not this guy who's in the streets. Ghost didn't want to go that direction completely, but he could go any direction he wants. He said, "you know what, Pretty Toney, that's the name for the bitches, and I'm going to wear my robe and my jewelry," which he enjoyed anyway. If you look at the cover of it, that picture was taken on stage during the tour for us to have album art. We had to take the picture onstage because we didn't have time to sit down in studio and take photos.

And regarding that single, Ghost is a huge fan of Missy, but did we necessarily want to lead with a radio record? No. He had all these street joints that we wanted to come with first. And we had a full mixtape of street shit that we wanted to push out first. And Def Jam was like, "No." And we were like, "Yo, let us do four videos with this mixtape of this grimy street shit."

Kevin Liles and Ghostface

We had it all written down. That'll get the streets on fire. Know that the Ghostface that they love is coming back. Then we'll drop the single.

Kevin Liles insisted on putting the glossy single ("Tush") out first. And Kevin told us in the office, "Lyor wanted you to come here. I didn't, because I'm not a fan, to be honest, of what you and Raekwon do. I'm not into that street shit. I'm into the radio hits." He told us that straight to our face, and Ghost said, "Nah, I respect that. But I'm going to tell you, I'm going to do what the fuck I do." And he kind of cursed him out and said, "Let's get the fuck out of here, Mike. Fuck this nigger." Just like that. And then he went to Lyor. That's when Lyor broke the news to him and said, "Ghost, just finish this project. You ain't going to have to deal with me or Kevin for much longer."

So Lyor did one album with us and then left to go to Warner. And that's when Jay-Z came in. He came in, and it was easy. We took our first and only meeting we needed to take with him, and he looked at us and goes, "Ghost, I love your music, keep doing what you do. Mike, don't break any album dates, don't bust any budgets, and I'll never, ever stop writing you checks." That's also when Lenny S came in, and he and John Kaslow started A and R and our projects from there. And they totally understood anything Ghost was speaking about.

Coincidentally, at the time the CFO at Def Jam was a guy named Joe Borrino, who I knew from Staten Island in high school. Not only did we have the blessing of the current president, but I had a CFO I was familiar with who looked at me and said, "Mike, all you got to fucking do is deliver records and don't break the fucking budgets, and we'll keep writing you checks."

For me, it was a very easy transition. For Ghost, it was a little frustrating because Lyor had a certain strategy, which was marketing, marketing, marketing, and forced students into the marketplace through distribution strategies.

Jay-Z and Ghostface

Then when Jay came in, he had an entrepreneur's mentality. Jay said, "here's your money, go do what you got to do and work with our team to do what you want to do." Why it became tougher for us to succeed in that model was because neither me nor Ghost nor even the Wu-Tang had a good rapport with radio at the time. They had already broken relationships with HOT 97 with Dirty at Summer Jam. So Wu-Tang music wasn't getting played on radio. Ghost really wanted a radio hit because everything was radio-driven back then.

At the same time, at the end of the *Supreme Clientele* tour, Eric Wilson was a touring agent at the time. He got on the call with me and Ghost, and he said, "Hey, coming out of *Supreme Clientele*, I want to do a thirty-city tour with you."

So I says, "Great."

He said, "The caveat to the tour is this. You, the Wu-Tang as a group, between leaving the Rage Against the Machine tour and management down at university having artists not show to shows, and taking advances but not following through, can't be late or miss any shows." He said I got to find a way to guarantee the shows, but I had thirty days to figure out how to do it.

Wilson calls me separately and says, "Mike, you're getting show offers. Will you guarantee the deposit, the first show, and after three or four shows when we are not late and on time, and we do the full shows with no issues, I could deposit for the rest of the tour. But will you guarantee some of the upfront money?"

Catch Ghostface Killah on tour:

10/2 Albany, NY- Northern Lights
10/3 Philly, PA- Trocadero
10/4 Carrboro, NY- Cats Cradle
10/5 Charleston, SC- Music Farm
10/7 Ft. Lauderdale, FL- Revolution
10/9 Oxford, MS- Lyric
10/10 Baton Rouge, LA- Spanish Moon
10/11 Austin, TX- Emos
10/13 Tucson, AZ- The Rock
10/14 Tempe, AZ- The Clubhouse
10/15 San Diego, CA- Canes
10/16 Los Angeles, CA Key Club
10/17 Santa Barbara, CA- Velvet Jones
10/19 Reno, NV- Club Underground
10/20 San Fran, CA- Slims
10/21 Arcata, CA- Arcata Theatre
10/22 Portland, OR- Berbati's Pan
10/23 Eugene, OR- WOW Hall
10/24 Seattle, WA- Showbox
10/25 Bellingham, WA- Nightlight
10/28 Salt Lake City, UT- Urban Lounge
10/29 Aspen, CO- Belly Up
10/30 Denver, CO- Bluebird
10/31 Boulder, CO- Fox

Ghostface tour dates, 2007

And I said, "sure." I didn't realize at the time it was forty grand in upfront money. But I did guarantee it. I took street money I had, gave it to Ghost for his deposits, nailed down the bus, did what we had to do. We made all the dates. So now we got a structure, and a guy who has a good touring reputation coming out of the Wu-Tang Clan.

When we went into *Bulletproof Wallets* and that tour, Eric comes back to me and he says, "Mike, we got a business decision to make. Linkin Park wants you to join their tour. It's sixty-two dates. The difference is, it's about half of the offer, maybe even less to be honest, than you're accustomed to getting. But it will open up the gates to a whole new marketplace for you guys."

I tell Ghost, "This is a good move to me." At first he struggled with it. Then I go, "Look, if I could offset your losses and replace what you believe you should be getting paid with a sponsor, will you do the deal?" And he said, "Yes."

I went and got Marc Ecko to print five thousand tour T-shirts for us at their cost. I got him to pay for the tour bus, fuel, floats, rental, and wrap the bus with his Ecko brand at his cost. We got a six-figure check on top of that for our pockets. Not only did Ghost make up the money he lost, he exceeded it.

Back of Ghostface / Marc Ecko watch

Now we do this sixty-two-date tour with Linkin Park. What that opened up for us was the underplays, and the rock-and-roll white-boy circuit of touring. Coming out of that project, we're touring, we're doing underplays after that, which are five hundred seats or less, but he was getting paid for three thousand seats, because the money made sense at the time because he was selling out rooms in advance.

Opening up this touring opportunity with the brand and entertainment associated with it really gave Ghost this reputation of being a touring artist. I then do all his paperwork to get him into Canada. He gets into Canada with the criminal record, we got past it. Now he's doing 120 to 140 tour dates a year. We went for nine years straight without canceling or missing a tour date ever. And then he got stuck in Europe because of a flight delay, had to come in through Chicago, New York, Chicago to try to get to Portland and missed his first festival in Portland. He got there at 12:10, and the curfew was midnight. And he got to do ten minutes of the gig, but it didn't count or was considered a cancellation. Otherwise, he would've still been on his roll of not canceling or missing shows.

Ghostface in Iceland, 2011

So going into the Jay-Z regime, after *The Pretty Toney Album*, their entrepreneurial ideology "go do what you do best." Def Jam as a company is looking at us going, "They're never on the radio, but they tour like a motherfucker throughout the country." What they were approving for us to do was take a hundred-grand at a pop out of the marketing fund, and instead of putting it toward radio, they were putting it toward paying for tour buses and hotel rooms for us. And Ghost loved that ideology. When you first present, "Oh, that's mint, that's great. I don't got to pay for my boss. I don't got to pay for rooms. The money that comes in, I'm paying you and my staff. Now I'm making an extra six figures plus."

The other thing I did was partnering him with his first branded partnership, which was Crown Royal Spirits. They paid $250,000 to sponsor a tour. Next thing you know, he's making, on a thirty-city route that any other Wu member was making about $10,000 a show, less cost, $5,000 in their pocket. He's making on average $25,000 a show, take home. He's making $600,000–$700,000 for thirty dates. Whereas other guys are making $60,000–$70,000. Because of the timing. Not because people didn't know what they were doing.

It's like the Adidas and ASICS shoes we released with cobranding. We did the mock out, co-branded specialty items. We did the doll, the Ghostface doll. I think it was selling anywhere from five hundred to fifteen hundred dollars a doll, packaged collectable. That was early on, too. That was in 2002 that we started those ideas. He has an energy drink that is definitively coming out, distributed by Circle K.

And all that solidifies our relationship. In a quick two or three years, all of a sudden he's like, "Fuck man, we're doing real business. We're making some real money." That's what solidified our relationship. I was showing him where the money was, and Jay-Z came in and they were like, "Go." We were just turning records. I didn't even have to see him. I'd just go to Borrino. "Borrino, open up another album budget."

"Okay, no doubt. What is it?"

"Two million."

"Okay, cool."

Gives us the advance, and now we're off and running. We opened our own studio, Def Jam's paying the studio bills and for the touring. We ended up doing, I think, seven albums with them until it ran out. We went through Jay-Z, L.A. Reid, and then the bank went dry when the music industry changed, let's call it. That's why there was that gap between *Bulletproof Wallets* and *The Pretty Toney Album*, partly because Ghost was touring so much, and partly the transition.

So *Toney* comes out, they do this thing, the show, the book, all that stuff. Then we moved to *Fishscale* and *More Fish*, two albums in one year. When I go back to what we recorded in Miami, he already recorded almost 75 percent of *Fishscale* in Miami during that lengthy time that we were there.

Money Comes First

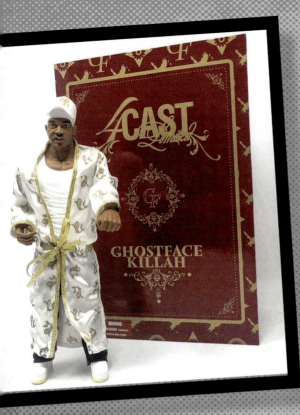

Ghostface limited edition doll

Wu-Tang energy drink

Ghostface-branded hat and shoes

Ghostface limited edition Adidas sneakers

And then, I'm not going to reveal how, but we got the masters to the "Summertime" Beyoncé record and we bootlegged it and released it. So now this is a hit record. This is how it became a hit record. It was an accident. Remember, there was a political agenda at HOT 97, specifically, led by Angie Martinez and Tracy, the head of programing at the time. Basically, Tracy said, "Ghost, fly to Italy. Spend two weeks with me. Bang me out and I'll make you the biggest musical artist in radio in New York." And Ghost said no.

And then, when Angie went on maternity leave, Sunny took her place on daytime radio. Sunny, the girl's name was Sunny. She's a cook now, a famous chef on the Food Network. She didn't know the politics.

Ghostface, Minya Oh, and Angie Martinez

So I send her the record. She breaks it on afternoon radio and plays it for a week or two. No one's really paying attention, because it wasn't in the program rotation, but Sunny was choosing to play it as her bonus record every day for a full week. And then the calls came in so fucking heavy to get the record played that it got added to rotation nationally overnight in one week. And the momentum on it was so out of control that even when Puff Daddy sent the cease-and-desist letter to HOT, all the stations were still playing the record, because it was supposed to be a Puff Daddy record. And then Jay and his team were like, "Hey, Beyoncé loves the record.

We're good with it." Beyoncé and Jay then invited Ghost to perform the "Summertime" record, and that's where we got the cover art for the album.

So for *Fishscale*, we knocked that project out. The album came out, did 108,000 units in its release week, which was good, considering there was no radio play, but the music was already being bootlegged heavily. By this time Jay-Z's out, and L.A. Reid's now here. So you went from a guy who wanted you to make what you want and get what you want to a guy who says, "I don't care what you're doing." L.A. Reid's ideology was about billing and numbers. He's an artist. Give the artist his money. But give me records to fill up my billing needs. That was his strategy in numbers.

He says to Ghost, "I need another album to fill a release date in December. I'll double your advance. I'll give you your next budget, and turn that in and I'll open up another budget at the top of the year, right behind it, at the same numbers." So it was a no-brainer.

More Fish was already in the computers. Every song in there was a leftover song from *Fishscale*. So from there I just put a bunch of features on the record and got that done. For Ghost, it was all second-string players. It was all records that didn't make *Pretty Toney* or *Fishscale*. They weren't trash records, but they were definitely not at the level he'd want to do all his own music at.

In retrospect, he wanted to get through the contract. And then, looking back at it now, we were lucky we had that contract. Because that was during the change in music and budgets. After we finished that contract, it was when the budgets changed. You went from seven-figure recording budgets to three-hundred-grand album budgets because of the change in music distribution. I know other artists of his caliber after the Def Jam period that went from half-a-million-dollar budget to record to a seventy-five-thousand-dollar budget to record. Budgets just started to end out. So people are like, man, fuck this. No one was releasing albums, they were just starting to switch over to streaming and the internet and everything. So we were lucky to have the budgeting we did and a guy like L.A. Reid saying to us, "I don't give a fuck." So in fact when we went on to do the next project (*The Big Doe Rehab*), we still had options.

After *Rehab* in 2007, Def Jam was pushing us hard to get more music. So we open the next budget. They asked, "Is there any other projects you could bring in the door and knock out?" *Wu-Massacre* we did under L.A. Reid's regime, which was Ghost, Rae, and Meth's album. And then we also did *GhostDeini the Great*, a collection of Ghost's greatest hits, so they could get another album out. So we started playing the billing game with them to push records out. At the same time, L.A. was like, "Ghost, do whatever the fuck you want."

At that same time, we were doing ten shows a year. We were making money in endorsements. We were making money with the record budget. Everything was good. And then the music industry just came to this slamming halt. So when we got to that last project that was due to L.A., that was *Apollo Kids*. All I had to do was find six or seven records that were originals, and the rest was a compilation of the hits, remixing those compilation hits. We did anything we could. We remixed "Run" with Lil Wayne. We put Ice Cube on another record. We just put records together over the last few years with a lot of the leftovers while he started writing *Supreme Clientele 2*. But the problem was the money wasn't there. Because after you're doing four or five billing albums and the first week's numbers aren't what they used to be, you can't get those same budgets, and you started to see diminishing returns.

Ghostface on tour

So, by that time, the budgets are changing, and I start changing strategy, which is, "All right. We're getting this money from albums because we're doing compilation hit albums." That's what the offering is for. We did the *Wu Block* project. We're doing all these mixtape albums to get bags of cash. He did this Adrian Young project (*Twelve Reasons to Die*). And because of all the touring we've done, we have a great reputation. The college tours, doing a lot of universities. Doing a lot of festivals because of the Linkin Park tour. He played Coachella four times himself. I'm doing all these festivals for him. I'm doing College Days for him. I'm getting fifteen to twenty things a year. So his touring is floating down to twenty to thirty grand a show, where in clubs it's down to like fifteen. So he's getting bags for mixtapes, waiting for the *Supreme Clientele 2* payday, and everything is changing.

But I landed him some of the touring deals with live bands at the time, to monetarily offset any of the losses, to make up for the change in the climate of music. And I take a gig working programming television, right? So, *Supreme Clientele 2* gets put on this back burner for two reasons. I've gotta take care of my family and pay my bills, so I take this TV gig. I'm still booking him on eighty shows a year. He's still got bag budgets to do these mixtapes. And we were just getting prepared to close this deal back at Def Jam for *Supreme 2* in 2013, we're talking about a budget, but I end up getting cancer, and I go down and I'm out of business for a good six to eight months. So it's kind of lost in the wind, not knowing what to do with his career. He's freestyling at this point with all these clowns around him, selling him their dreams.

So just before that, until the current timeframe, until now we're finally getting offers of millions for *Supreme 2*. It's come back full circle, the demand and the music, let's call it. And look at how music's changed now. You got all these kids putting it up on their SoundClouds and social sites to build a business. And then get popular, then selling music to millions of people directly. So it completely changed everything.

Regarding television and film appearances, we had another agent who was lining all of that up. Of course, that business is not without its complications. For example, Jon Favreau, and you can quote me on this, screwed us on the *Iron Man* music portion of the business, him and his music team screwed Ghost for millions on the music piece. Because Jon had a partnership with the music placement in *Iron Man* through either a satellite business or whatever he was dealing. And turned in a song for the *Pretty Toney* piece on the airplane. And it was last-minute and we were getting it in last-minute, and we replayed it with a band because apparently the DJ sampled something that we didn't have the right clearance for.

So we replayed it with a band, submitted it to him. He gets it in, but they give us performance payment and royalties only. We went back and I bitched to his team and they said, Jon won't approve the sync for you. If you get sync, every time it's played, everywhere it's getting played, you're getting the royalties. If you get performance, you're getting a prorated minimal royalty place in the movie. So the difference between Ghost making just about six figures on

Money Comes First

the song placement versus sync licensing, which would've made him millions, was because Jon Favreau got greedy. He burned us for over two million bucks. Now maybe people around him didn't explain to him why or what he was doing. But ultimately they said he said, "No, I won't switch it to his sync. Sorry we made the mistake, but it's done."

So now, this guy, and I'm not going to say exactly who, because this guy broke an NDA and said, well, remember when Ghost was on set, he spent the day there, shot a scene with Downey at the pool. Ghost plays Iron Man, and that was supposed to be like an inside joke for the movie. And then they were going to play the song in the film as well. For whatever reason, they wanted to cut the pool-party scene out of the film. Jon called the next day and said, "Hey, Ghost. I'd like you to come back today. I know we didn't have you. We had you yesterday on set for fifteen hours and we shot one hour. This is Hollywood. We got another idea of you standing on the beach with Downey as Iron Man. Will you come back and do it?

At the time, though, Ghost, because we were on set fifteen hours, and he was exhausted, and his sugar went down while he was on set, we didn't take care of it properly. So he was really sick the next day, his sugar levels were off, he didn't get proper sleep. He was elevating his feet because his calves were aching. And he had to decline going back on set. So one of the guys who worked closely with Favreau said the only reason Ghost didn't get a sync on that song is because he never came back to set that day. And Ghost was like, "I told the motherfucker I was sick. My diabetes was acting up. Any other day you want, I can come back."

The MF Doom album is still completed. I talked to his people the other day, and the wife is almost treating it like it's going to be some rare collectible that she'll decide to put out when she's ready. And he can't excise any kind of control over that basically. Ghost got paid cash to record his part, which he took in lieu of being involved with the business at the time.

Supreme 2 is done, he finished it. We're negotiating the release platform now, put it that way. We may blockchain it. We're not sure. It's like with the NFT I mentioned earlier, I explained to Ghost the importance of innovating and being prepared for the future.

CHAPTER 13

BLACK JESUS

Yo, hit me for these Tommy Hill, ice rockin' niggas
Peace, this summer's mines, I blow the biggest
Back up off me, while I grab my dick and hold the Heini
Park the Blue 600, Wally Kings is right behind me
Tackle clubs, never rock Lugz, I'm way above
This mic is like the Golden Gloves verses spark plug
It's like the pennant, seminar's the play-off
Start the day off like Cochran got OJ off
The specialist who eyeballed the mistress necklace
Perpetuous, this curly head kid's treacherous
Let go the echo, so we can dip dip dive the gleego
Throwin' can-can, eat that plus this instrumental
Awwww shit, say Stark-oligist, Starks-oligist
Fried fish halibut
Pull out the bull horn
and celebrate like Kunta was born
We elbowed our way inside Loud and got on
I played the building, burn a branch and get filled in
Like Pilgrims G-in' Pepperidge Farms from out a millions
Who wanna rhyme? Who wanna challenge the swordman?
That rock that fisherman hat like Gorton's

I'm a spiritual person. I believe that everything happens for a reason. I believe you got to go through hell to come out right, and nobody in those projects would ever know I was the one that had that lotto ticket. I had to work for it. When I started traveling and all the other shit. It's like we were probably the worst off in that building, and then God just kept me on the path where I could become the star of the building.

That road, it wasn't easy. I always seen, after a while, like in the '80s, I saw myself being where I'm at right now, like being on stage, because after a while we started rhyming and break dancing and everything else. I knew I was going to be there. I knew I was going to be there somewhere. I just felt it . . . I saw it. God kept me on that path where whatever I saw, I achieved it. You only go as far as you can see. If you can't see past the bullshit and see yourself, or how you want to, then you're probably never going to make it there.

> "But my journey on that particular road was also a long one. Back in the day, we were going to church, but then I got introduced to Islam in the '80s. Even so, it really didn't start playing a big part in my life until about '87 or '88."

My uncle, remember the one I told you was crazy, getting drunk all the time. His name was Islam, he was a good dude. He introduced me to Islam when I was fourteen years old. He was a Five Percenter, and he'd just walk through the projects. "You'd better not be eating no pork. Yo, you need to get these lessons." You see him coming in to talk to us, me and my man Burto and a few of the guys. But a lot of Godbody was hitting in Staten Island. That's how you come with the Rakims, like RZA was Rakeem, you know that I mean? And Raekwon. And me and my older cousin, he locked up right now, though. But they'd come around and start dropping gems and all of that like that or whatever.

One thing just led to the next. It opened my mind to a lot of things. It didn't really kick in all the way until I started really hanging around a bunch of the rest of the Godbody. That's when it really started getting more, and more, and more, and more. He used to tell me, "Black man is God. Don't eat no pork, stay away from that pork shit." At fifteen, sixteen, I started leaving that pork alone. That's the first thing I changed. I noticed that every time I ate pork, I'd get a stomachache. A ham and cheese always sounded good, but then when I'd eat it I'd be like, "Damn, why the fuck is my stomach hurting?"

And it just grew on you. That Islam, the Five Percent just grew on you. And these is lessons that you need in your life to really understand life. It was like they was giving you knowledge. Then you getting a chance to know, to awaken yourself. If you was a person that was asleep, you know what I mean, that you didn't have no knowledge of nothing, this mathematics, these one hundred and twenty questions and answers and all that will wake you up. To know who you was, who you was as a person, and why you're here in America and dealing with all this and how much this land is yours, and you know what I mean? Open it up like that, because mathematics is everything, because one plus one always going to equal two regardless. There is no, like, how Jay-Z said, numbers don't lie, people do. So everything adds up, you know what I mean? I flew under that flag for a minute, and I still bring Islam into my life because it's a way of life. Mathematics is a way of life. Islam is a way of life.

Converting to Islam shaped my life tremendously. Right now it's like I'm so humble, I feel God. I feel Him. I know He exists. Through my dreams, through everything. Down to His angels. Once you get more closer and more spiritual, the more humble you become.

My mind is like a spiritual mind. So I'm more in spirit all the time. I like to look at shit and be like, "Oh, so that's why that happened like that. Because you went and did that," like calculate. I'm more a calculated person spiritually. Like Islam is one, "I'm a Muslim, dead Godbody." But Islam is Islam.

That's what led me to become Muslim. I went going through that way, going through the Five Percent way. So that's what led me to become Muslim, because I was already in Islam. So when I got a chance to go into the mosque, and feel what it felt like to stand in front of the imam and pray in my heart, not knowing, and walked out there being clean. It's like, "Oh, okay. I get it." And it was a certain revelation just came to me.

So throughout my years . . . I went to church before. In my later years, I find myself going to the mosque. When I leave that mosque, I felt a different way. I felt a certain feeling come over me. That's just for me, because everything ain't for everybody. But I felt clean. I felt in my spirit that I had belonged there, like that's where Allah wanted me to be. I felt that, in that mosque, and I never felt a feeling like that no other place but that place right there, you know what I mean?

So I learned, I got more in tune with myself, through the mathematics, through Islam, and through spirituality. I started to learn myself more. So now when something's telling me to do something, now I don't even question it. Yo, if I feel in my heart it's right, then it's right. If I feel it's wrong, it's wrong. I can't steal anything from nobody, not even a book of matches, because I feel like, "Why did I take that?" You might give me extra money back from the store at the cash register, you can give me an extra twenty dollars, yo, I got to give it back because it feels like I'm taking something that's not mine. Even though I could blame it on, "Oh, the white man been taking from us for years." But I don't go in that way. I know what I do here, I'm going to be questioned on the day of judgment. So what I'm doing here on this earth now, I'm trying to make sure my good outweighs my bad. I did a lot of fucked up shit, you know what I mean?

And that sticks. So I stuck in that mosque with the imam, and took the *shahada* and all this stuff like that, and learned more about Islam. There is so much you can learn about Islam and the prophets. I could've read Donald Goergen's books and all these other books and Iceberg Slim, but only certain things make me want to read it, open my mind, and when I'm reading about things dealing with Islam or some type of knowledge, or reading about the prophets and all that stuff like that, I get a kick out of that. That's what opens me up. I like that.

I got to feel connected to what I'm reading, because in my mind, I'm here in the physical, but mentally I'm not here. When I could talk to a person it's like I'm on another frequency. I don't believe a lot of beliefs that people believe. Like I said, I believe in it, on the day of judgment. I believe everything I did in my life I will get questioned. I don't believe just because you die you're automatically in heaven, unless you was an innocent one. Like the innocent babies, or like my two brothers who died that never robbed or stole. I believe they're sitting in front of their heaven door, even though heaven and hell is here on earth, but in Islam it says, "On earth as it is in the heavens." So there is more heavens. There's more heavens above. This ain't just the heaven that we're here, here. This world is so big. There's layers of heavens, second heaven, third heaven, fourth heaven, fifth heaven, sixth heaven, seventh heaven. The righteous ones that will make it to that seventh or eighth heaven up there like that, it's like, "Yo, you got to really, really be on your shit to get there." Even if I die, if you place into heaven, I don't want to have that heaven where it's like a report card. You're just passing with a sixty-five, now you're in a Days Inn, you know what I mean? Like, "All right, man, you mentioned a hotel, but you in a motel." So I want to stay in the Ritz-Carlton. I want to be there. I want my clean sheets and AC crazy like that. I want to eat the best of the best foods. So I'm trying my best to live a life of trying to do good deeds and clean up my old bad deeds. I want to fit in there. You want to pass your test with eighty, eighty-five and better, especially nineties, really. So it's like, "Yo, you know what? I want to be in the nearness of Allah. I want to be in His nearness and the oneness, and the oneness."

Like that. So whatever I got to do to make the Most High happy, I'm going to do it. I'm going to do whatever I got to do to make Him happy. I'll do it. I'm not perfect. But in my heart it's like, "Yo, I don't care what it is for the Most High, if I can get ahead and just to get a nice smile out of Him," if Allah do smile. Now I believe Allah smiles, and I believe Allah gets mad. Because you really can't have one without the other. But whatever I could do to touch His energy, that's what I want to live for like that. You don't have to be a Christian or Muslim just to be righteous. I want to get that on the record. You could be righteous as long as your heart and your intentions are righteous, and you're living that, then you're righteous.

But you will, by the time you die, you will be questioned in the grave. Who was your God? Who did you follow? And things of that nature, so I just want to be clear for the people that's out there, you will be questioned about everything you did on this planet. And the planet, the years is short, you know what I mean? They say one day, what they say, is like a thousand years, but a thousand years is like one day. I forgot how it goes, but by the time you get to be in your eighties or nineties, this time going to been done flew so fast, it's like, "Yo, where'd it go?" And it's over. It's over for you. So you got to get your shit together right now.

So I believe in all the prophets. I believe in Jesus and all that like that. I believe he's one of many miracles. From Adam to Noah, you learn from these prophets on what they had did. You learn from these prophets and stuff like that, you learn how to live your life once you're very in tune. It's certain things I could feel coming to me that haven't even happened yet. But then when it does arrive, it's like, "Yo, you know what? I felt that. I knew it." That's what that was. Because it's in you already. You're in tune. You feel something's going to happen.

I know when there's a full moon out all the time, because it has me feel a certain kind of way. Anxious, anxious and stuff like that. Because the sun and the moon have the attractive powers over the planet. So once the moon is receiving all of the light from the sun, it has an effect on our planet. Once the full moon comes, they call it a luna, right? So the full moon's a luna, it has the attractive powers over our planet. You have the people kind of going crazy a little bit, that's why crime is up around the time of a full moon. You send more police out on full moons if you noticed. But that "luna" is only short for "lunatics," because motherfuckers going crazy.

I ask myself a lot of questions about how I view things differently from other people. I'm just trying to figure this world out. I'm the type of person to be like, "Yo, just because I could walk around and we could be driving around and do all this other shit, you got to remember we still in space." We are on a planet that is spinning so fast the gravity is holding us down. We're spinning. Times when I think it's like, wow, so I'm on this planet here. Okay. Listen, this planet over here, the Most High made it, gave us water, gave us trees. Even when I'm in the plane, when I look down and I'm flying over a bunch of trees, the trees look like broccoli to me. The trees are looking like broccoli because they got the regular leaves on the top and that's how broccoli is. This planet is green. All the forest and the trees and all that, and you have water. So when I'm looking out the plane window, I'm looking like, damn. My mind just travels like, wow, so this thing is shaped like that and it got to be good for you because the trees give off oxygen. But then they say broccoli is like one of the best alkaline foods for your body and all the obvious shit like that. Like eat your greens, eat your greens, eat your greens.

This world is populated with a lot of green, even under the water. The color green it's under the water because it's plant life under there. When you say the water is blue, it's like, no, that's just the reflection from the sunlight. If the sun is yellow or orange or whatever you want to call it, just say the sun is yellow, and you got green under the water. Say the water is clear but you got green under there like plant life. When you take your crayons and you mix green and yellow together, what's that make? Green and yellow makes blue. And that's the reflection from the sky. That just . . . hits the water and it goes right back up in the sky, that makes your sky blue. Because in reality the sky has no color probably, which I know is like, it's no color but it's the reflection.

But you see where my mind goes. The way I think is just different. I got a different way of thinking about life, about where I'm going to go after life. I think about how I came in. I think about how I chose my life before I was even born. To take on whatever I'm going through in this life, whether it's sickness, and all that stuff like that—I chose this. And God gave me character and gave me awareness. A lot of times, I'm not even on this planet, but I'm on this planet.

> "I think about a lot of things. I like science and I like just the prophet stories, and the prophets, and the angels, and the people of the beginning. Those are the things that turn me on. I don't want to think about a lot of things that everybody else sits at home and thinks about."

Just things, man, my mind just it goes like, even like oh shit, you hearing your own voice while you speak. Like, "Damn, how the fuck do the Most High?" You think like, He gave me a voice, He gave us hands. If you got one hand missing, don't you know how difficult that shit is? How would you fuck around? How would you tie your sneakers? Like you tying your shit, you got to fuck around and try to put your shoes on anyway. Like you could take a dude that got no arms, like, damn, how the fuck do he put his pants on? Or how is he feeding himself? Things like that. I respect the people that got body parts missing and they still out here doing what they do.

That's why I respect Stevie Wonder. That's one of my favorite artists, but he's blind. He's blind, but he's talking about a ribbon in the sky, but he never even probably seen a ribbon. My mind just goes to things like that.

I might get up out the bed and I feel like, thank you. Thank you, God. Allah. All praises due to Allah. Because I could be able to stand that day. Some people can't get out the bed and just stand. You understand what I'm saying? I'm mindful that I got legs and I got hands that grab that. If you lose a pinky or a thumb, God made you so perfect, if you lose one thing that He had made for you, you going to feel that.

Because right now you tying your sneakers, you belting your backpack, you making your bed, you grabbing a fork. Nigga, you ain't got no fucking thumb. It sucks that you can't do without using your fucking thumb. How are you going to wash the dishes? How are you going to fuck around and eat properly? You have food falling all over the place. God gave it to you like that. That's where my mind be. So when you say about your spirit. I never really just looked and see how my spirit was, but you know, I'm an analyzing person.

I changed my ways so much over the years. I always had a humble soul. It's just that the streets have raised me, and it just is doing a lot of crazy shit. But at times I did crazy shit. That's how I know that Allah was next to me because I will feel bad when I did it as I did it. Like, it'll come over me like, "Damn, why you do that?" A lot of shit I done did in my life to people, if I had a chance, I'd apologize to them because that was little-kid shit. Doing shit, people I stuck up, people I robbed, people I cut. Where I am at right now, I feel embarrassed for the shit I did.

And I did so much shit that I can't even tell my family that I did certain shit and my friends and shit like that, because it seemed like it's a sin just for me to repeat the worst of the shit that I had done to people. I got to hold it. That question is, when it comes to that time when Allah has to ask me, because the angels already know, it's already in my paperwork with the angels. The Most High will come to me and ask me why I did this and that, and I can't lie to Him. This has to be the truth. And my truth is, I was young, this was my environment, and this was my mentality. Because if I would've knew before, I had been spiritual like that, I wouldn't have did it. That's what it is. So, bro, my spirituality is just me. That's it. The way I think.

Because once you repent and you be like, "Yo, Allah, may you forgive me for the things that I have done," and you pray and asking the prophet Muhammad, "May Allah's choices, blessing and peace be upon him, to beg for you to the Most High, to forgive you for your sin," and stuff like that. If you would have known correctly at that time, but you was an adolescent, you was a teenager, you was just going wild because of your environment. Sometimes we don't mean to do the shit that we do.

Even if somebody tried to tell you right from wrong at that time, when you dealing with that . . . it's like, you can have kids, they get to a certain age and they won't listen until they go through it. You got to touch that stove to see if it's hot. If I told you, "Do not touch the stove," okay, I'm telling you, but if you touch it and you burn yourself, then it's on you. So you have to learn by

Black Jesus

experience. This is what you call life experience. You have to learn, a man or woman has to learn on their own to go through that shit like that. Some people get killed. You can get killed in the midst of learning.

In this world, you got to understand what you're looking for. That's why they say, "Love, peace, and happiness." Happiness is the ultimate of everything in your life that you could be looking for. Even when I pray and stuff like that, yo man, I ask for good health, long life, happiness. If you got love . . . got to have love, and once you've got love, you've got peace, and then once you're at peace, you're happy. Love, peace, happiness. It's not happiness, peace, love. No, it's love, then peace, then happiness. At the end of the day, regardless if you're rich or you're poor, you just want happiness in life.

I'm a firm believer of karma. What goes around comes around because everything has a balance. Everything. You got right, you got wrong. You got weak, you got strong. You got your left side of your brain, you got your right side of your brain. You got your left eye, your right eye. Left leg, right leg. Everything has a balance here. So what goes around is going to come around. That's just straight karma. That's just the balance right there. They might say the ying and the yang. Hot and cold. You got love and hate. It's two things. I believe things come back to you and if you doing good things, I believe that things that come back good, come back good on you. When you do good deeds, you do bad deeds, bad deeds are come. It's like that. But like when people come in the world, somebody's got to die. Each time somebody is born, a baby got to die, somebody's got to die. Because if it don't happen that way, shit, the earth might fall out of space somewhere or fall from its place because it'd be overpopulated, but the Most High knows, like, this is the weight of the earth and this what needs to be here, to maintain anything more might tilt the earth or whatever.

Yeah. But God knows everything. He's the creator. The creator of everything. He knows what He has created. He knows this. Before it was created, He knew what He was creating and He knew that He was going to create it. So somebody's born, somebody's got to go. That's just the science of life. That's just how it works. From the beginning. Right now, we are on our last days. These are our last days. But you know what? We'll see in that day of judgment because a lot of nonbelievers don't believe in the day of judgment.

I believe there's a day of judgment because all of us would have to get judged for everything that we do. I had two brothers with muscular dystrophy, and I believe they're sitting in front of the heaven door or maybe in heaven. They just might be excused and just go straight to the heavens because they never stole, they never had sex with a woman, and things like that. If you don't have no sins on you, you don't have to be judged. You're excused.

Now, for everybody that's thinking that grandma is in heaven right now and looking down on you, man that's bullshit. I don't believe that. I believe she's in a resting place. Or my grandfather. I don't care what rapper died. Oh, he's looking down on you. How do you know this nigga's in heaven? Because there's so much foul shit this nigga sitting there in hell did. You understand me? It could have been your mother. I don't care how sweet your mother was to you. Your mother could have had somebody else killed before.

But you see how I think? Your mother could have had somebody killed. Grandmother was so sweet, but she set this motherfucker up and robbed them and had him killed. But you don't know that, you think your grandma is grandma. "Oh, that's my grandma, she could never do something like that." Grandma could have been a hoe, a freak, a fucking bank robber, any fucking thing. That's why I say that everybody has to be judged, and everybody will get judged on Judgment Day. When the earth and everything is finished, we will get judged on that day for your asking your deed.

That's why I tell people, like, "Yo, man, you're good in this world that you do right now because we just living for today, but I know the future." And I look at death and I'd be like, "Yo, what about when you here?" Like, right now, we don't even walk around thinking about what it's going to be like when you transition into the next shit, when God takes your life. Like, what's it going to be like, not saying wherever you go, but just in the mix of going. What's that going to feel like when you leaving? You don't even sit down and think about that. Are you ready? Are you prepared at any time? Because they say God can take your life at any time. He can take your life five minutes from now, ten minutes from now, a year from now, a second from now, but are you prepared in your mind to know that you're about to make this transition, just to go on to somewhere else like that, and what is it going to be like while you're transitioning into that other part.

It's, like, people don't think like that. They just think they waking up to wake up and going to sleep to sleep. But there is going to be that day, the final day, when that shit come to pass, what are you going to do? There's nothing you can do. You see what I'm saying? So if you're going to get judged, like my brothers, they didn't do nothing. And I had a daughter that passed away. She was a twin. But she had passed away like a couple of days after birth because her bowels was clogged up and stuff like that. She only lived for four or five days, then she passed away.

But they go right to their place. We all going to have to get questioned. What did you do? What did you do with your life? What do you do with your money? How did you treat your mother? How did you treat your father? The angels got everything written down. If I killed somebody in front of a tree, that tree will be a witness for God that, yes, he murdered him right under me. Your hands become like that. Your hands become witnesses. Your body is going to be a witness to the murder or any crime that you had committed. And if people don't understand that . . . And besides Ghostface the rapper, that's where my mind is at.

But I'm just saying the world is so wicked. You got these people that run the world that are so wicked that did this. They just doing anything right now. The watermelons ain't the same watermelons we ate when we was young. There's no black seed in the watermelon. There's no seed in the oranges. So I'll look at the bananas, the bananas, looking like us. This shit is big. It's big—bananas is never that big. So everything we eating right now, the majority is fake food. It's everything is fake. When I was young, cereal tasted so good. When I was eating McDonald's when I was little, it tasted mad good, because it was the real ingredients. Now you might stop and get a shake from Burger King or McDonald's, the shake could feel so light. But back then it was heavy. What did y'all do to the ice cream? Why does it feel so light? And the cereal, it don't even taste right. Apple Jacks don't taste the same no more, Trix don't taste the same no more. None of that shit tastes the same no more. Where's this world going to?

"So this is what I think about when I'm telling you, God is only maybe one hundred and fifty years or less out of here. Two hundred, the most, that I really feel in my spirit. I think it goes no more. I think it goes no more because everything is happening. Earthquake, tsunami, viruses."

Now they're talking about shortages of this and shortages of that. You got certain continents, like Africa, it's snowing over there. You know what I mean? Where in certain places it's snowing. And then it's like, yo, I remember one time I went to Texas, it was snowing in Texas. It was like, "Oh, what the fuck is this about?" When you can't even tell the difference from the seasons no more, the last days is here for real, real. So I feel sorry for my great, great grand—because even for my grandchildren now, they're going to be living in some shit. And it makes you . . . Sometimes I don't really want to have no more children because you don't want them to see this shit. But it's like, yo, we're in a time that we're really, really fucked up. We're fucked up.

This is where the world is at right now. This is serious shit. And I give thanks to the Most High, almighty Allah, for making me aware in this lifetime, just to have a witness. I'd rather be poor and broke with a bunch of knowledge, to have awareness, than to be rich and to be dumb as a motherfucker. To be sitting up with fifteen, sixteen million and be illiterate. It's like, "Yo, no, wait, I don't want to be in that." And I thank Allah. Every time I get a chance to think about him making me aware. I got to give thanks. Because you have to. My awareness so I could warn my family, warn my babies of what's coming and shit like that. Yo, that's the biggest thing to me, that I accept that, I'll take that more than anything right now. Because right now you got all these motherfuckers with money they can't do nothing with it. What you going to do? You got millions of dollars right now nigga, you can't even buy a can of Lysol. Because there's no Lysol in the fucking stores.

It's all being done by men, mankind. Everything is happening right now is mankind going against the will of God, going against the laws of God. You want to try to go to space like you going to run, you building up all these other shit, you fucking up our food. It's all done by man. The ozone layer was just fucked up a minute ago. The ozone layer fucked up. That's what caused these tsunamis and the earthquakes and all that shit. Because it's like, yo, the thing in the earth, now you all got shit where you all could play with the weather and all that, all this is done by mankind. And it's the higher-ups, because the poor people, we don't know how to do all this shit. We're not bringing guns and shit in here. It's the people that run the world. It's the people that have got all the money that run the banking system, that run the world, the media, they entertain all this shit.

We don't have none of that shit. We don't know how to get that shit. We don't have to bring guns across the boat and do all this other shit and cocaine across the boat and letting it sit here like that. We don't know how to do all that shit. It's a plot for us to kill each other. And that's why, as a people, we have to understand like, "Yo, nah." These old motherfuckers that's running this shit. Come on, man. It's not right.

And you know that, because all this is like seventy-, eighty-year-olds, they live in old traditions. They still got their slavery mentality, that master mentality. When the new people started getting in the White House or wherever, like just started being in power, younger people didn't have that mentality. The ones with the good hearts, we could start seeing, "Yo, okay, yo, this ain't right." But as long as you got the motherfuckers that's been, "Keep the Hispanics out of here, keep them Blacks out of here. Let's keep it down. And this that and that. We got to do this. Yo, we can make more money by selling them synthetic drugs than the real shit."

> "Like the cure for AIDS might be one of these vegetables or fruits, but they're not going to tell you that. They're going to shut you down and be like, 'Yo, you're selling fake news.' When it's like, yo, you don't want to take all the motherfuckers because once you start taking one drug for AIDS or whatever, you're taking them every day, that's going to fuck with your liver or your kidney. When the gods made every medicine here for us in the fucking earth that we needed for our body to fight off whatever."

So, yeah. It's like, "yo, I've been blessed." I grew up really poor. I always been that diamond in the rough, to come out of that situation. And I never forget that. That's why it's all praises due to the Most High all day. You cannot stop saying "Thank you, God." You're not even supposed to stop saying that. But because you thank God for every second that you live or millimeter of a second, even take ten seconds ago, that's a blessing, God had given you another. It's like, yo, because you could have passed away ten seconds ago. You could have had a heart attack. When you walked across the street, you didn't get hit by a car. You don't say thank you. After you finish your food, you don't say thank you. When you receive your food, you don't say thank you. For you to have your sight, you don't say thank you. For you to have a body part, thank you. You know how many times you supposed to say thank you?

We're not promised tomorrow to wake up. Because anything can happen. So there's a blessing. There's a blessing and that blessing is God, man. Is Allah, is God, whatever God you got is that, because God is one. He has many names. He has ninety-nine names. But it's a blessing, however you put it.

I love everything. I don't even like killing—I don't kill spiders. If I did catch a bug, for the most part, I would let the bug crawl on a piece of paper and put them outside the door or window. Because at the end of the day, everything has—listen, man, I got red blood, and so do a lot of insects. You would kill a fly and the fly, you see red blood on the wall. It's its blood. We got the same blood. But I get it, though, some animals might need to be killed. Especially if you're in a jungle when a fucking lion is trying to eat your ass, you've got to defend yourself. Just make sure you ask for forgiveness for whatever you killed. Because they got families they got to feed, too. So it's just like that. Just be mindful. Be mindful of the things that you do. Nothing goes unnoticed here on this planet with each individual. Certain animals . . . I don't touch them. I throw a mouse out the window or just put them outside.

Even with people. I have to help people. I have to feed people. To this day I got people all through Africa that I feed now. Still. Since I've been there in '97. Still feed the people. Help them build a mosque. Building mosques out there. This is what I do. I don't really work for me, I work for the Most High. I work for Allah. Allah is my God. This is what I do it for. I do it for him because I want my scale. I believe in the seven heavens. If there is a seven heavens, I want to stay in the Waldorf Astoria. Put me there, if I did enough deeds to make it there. But, but, but, I understand you can pass on your report card with a sixty-five. That's passing. So you might just get into heaven based on you just passed. It's like if there is seven of them, I want to see how it feels to sit next to the Father in the most glorious of heavens, and there is six different hells. There's six different hells. There is hell so cold it feels hot, or so hot it feels cold. Either one of those like that. It's six different ones, other than just the fire. I don't want me or my family to be there. When you turn Muslim, you allow seventy of your people to be in heaven with you. Just like right now, if I got you to convert today or tomorrow to Islam and you take your jihad, you automatically enter the heaven. You and the seventy people that you want to take with you.

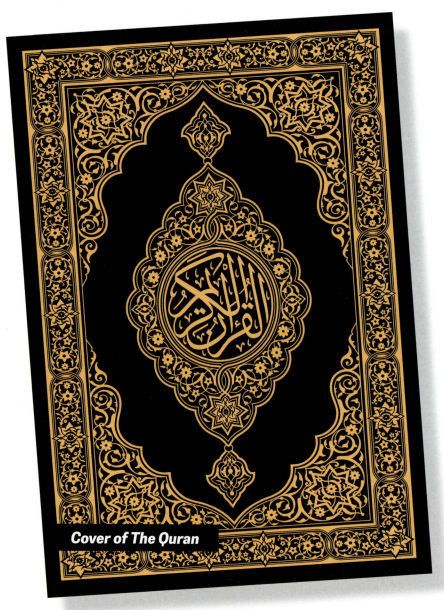

Cover of The Quran

Be aware that there's somebody always watching you when you think they're not watching. And there's angels all around. Even right now there's angels around us taking notes of what I'm telling you. There's angels right now sitting with you right there. So you have to be mindful. We have to learn. It's hard, though, because we always sinning. Even when we're cursing, we're sinning, when you curse. But we have to be mindful of these things so we can ask forgiveness. And that shit's hard, though.

So there's many avenues that we can go. This is so much that the Most High had placed over me to me. Like I said, He gave me that awareness and He gave me the knowledge and the wisdom to understand things. To understand is the best part. It's like, I understand why the people that's doing these things to us in the world because they're devils. You got all kinds of devils. The devil is someone that does the opposite of God. And they're doing bad things because God is all. God created the devil. But the devil is sent here to do the devil's work. So you really can't get mad at the devil nowadays because he's just doing his work.

The devil is busy. So you've got to sound like, "Yo, stay off this motherfucker's way." Like, yo, "Okay, you doing it? But keep that shit over there," because anybody that wants to kill a nation and they kill population off, yo, that's the bad devil. That's the real wicked bad, bad, bad devil. God created the devil. And at the end of the day, devil's going to be under God. At the end of the day, when it's all said and done, God going to check and put His creation in check in and that's it.

So that's why on earth right now it's a battle between God and devil. When you see all these wars and this and that, it's a battle. Who's going to get more followers? The devil is doing his numbers. He's getting followers every day. You see what I'm saying? So it's just what team you on? Are you team God or you team devil? That's it. So what team you on? What shirt you got? What jersey you wearing? What helmet you got on? What you playing for? And that's how I think.

CHAPTER 14

MALCOLM

Aiyo, I'm like Malcolm, out the window with the joint
Hoodied up, blood in my eye, I let two fly like fuck it,
look how these niggas duck shit
One kid hollering "what!" lookin' up, he the big wig
Fake ass cat, low life, sodomize mind
Beatin' niggas, big bricks of bread, sell 'em as dimes
His feet hurt, networking he get no work
Yo smack him where his hand hurt, fuck what he worth
Yo he sucked his thumb, slew-footed kid, laced with the big gums
Stuntin' to my Baltimore niggas that he on the run
Plus he ill in the drums, heartburn for life, calcium man
Watch him grab the Tums, he's a front
Pigeon-toed Tyler's sister with the fat ass
Show hash for Hines up the block plus he smashed her
Big Buck did him something deadly, act premeditated
Buck 60 strike was the medley
Nights like Van Halen, seen him at the tunnel with his skin peeling
Did two days thought he was jailing
You get close, look at his hands
That's the same kid that cut his wrists, talking 'bout "the cuffs did it"

He bantam weight, fronting majorly, eyes like Sammy Davis, Jr.
Rounded off with a fade, G, he sport the Bob Hope classics
Ran down Asics, Kmart, the short sleeve shit be the basics
He eat hams, shitted on himself twice
Big-hatted Jews rushed the nigga out in Crown Heights

[Chorus]
Yo let me show you how the game go
We getting rid of all the prostitutes
Tony wants the streets back fo' sho'
Too many hustlers, too many thieves
We're fuckin' up, who's willin' to fight and teach the seeds
Too much TV, guns and robberies
Lust and greed and hate the four devils' jealousy

Yo, I-cham punched Mase in his face over some bullshit
The other night they kidnapped his brother, pokin' it with knives
It's raining, 85 degrees, kinda muggy
One of the nights they throw in his face it's real ugly
Yo, we up in Jonesy's posin', all these niggas know me

From fucking wit' Un and these niggas, heavy parolees
Yo, we played the speaker
And from a distance we could see these chains
The piece laid flat on his chest, was two planes
Ashy hands yo, no need for rings at all
He just cracked the V8 backed up, leaned against the wall
Look at Flower, he just came home, he on like a fuck
Did a dime for holding up the gods up in the armored truck
Ten years later son 280 on the weight tip
He throwing up six plates plus he studied Matrix
He's a wally horse shout it out sweatin' through his velour
Cock-eyed nigga back up his neck, he had sores
Sammy eagerly rode up on him
Toxi off the turkey with the joint on him
"Flower, look, his man stood up before him"
The bitches hit the table, Jah King stripped off his cables
Shots went off, Sam'll get a chance to make his debut
Flower grabbed Tiff, his man with the sideburns, hat fell off
We nerd his wig worms, he hid behind Rich
C Allah hit the light switch, young girls were trampled
In the men's room, Poo pistol-whipped Mase, and broke the handle
Desperate, crawling to the door on all fours
Cham kicked the jukebox, the theme song rode in was "It's Yours"
Oh my goodness, Ba grabbed the Mo bottle, thrashin'
He layin' like a gay model shouting out "Sebastian!"
He smiled with his teeth missin, beggin' for mercy

"No more, God, there's 68 thousand down at pier three"
Out came the cannon, whistled out zaggin'
Cham snatched his flag, four big rocks, enter the dragon
It's over, another story told
Lying with the snakes, tongue kissin' cobras

Yo let me tell you how the game go
We getting rid of all the prostitutes
Tony wants the streets back fo' sho'
Too many hustlers, too many thieves
We're fuckin' up, who's willin' to fight and teach the seeds
Too much TV, guns and robberies
Lust and greed and hate the four devils' jealousy

Malcolm

> "Racism is fucked up. Because we as a people, why it got to be racist? Why it got to be the Black race or the white race. I don't care what color you is. But why do the higher people . . . let's ask the question for a second. Why do the higher authorities . . . because you know the Black man and the Puerto Rican man, we don't really haven't got a voice for this."

Even when America started, like for instance, I was telling my friend, this is simple. You say why is it when you bake a cake, and you got all types of cake . . . So why the angel food cake got to be white? And why the devil's food chocolate cake got to be black or brown. Why did the black jellybean got to be one of the nastiest jellybeans inside the package?

We ain't never seen a motherfucker on a hundred-dollar bill. You take a hundred-dollar bill, who the fuck is that? Ben Franklin? He wasn't even the fucking president. He had money. How the fuck he got his little fat-ass face on a hundred-dollar bill?

Abraham Lincoln. They acting like Abraham Lincoln tried to free the slaves and going to put them on a penny, on the brown thing and shit. The penny, he could still have a regular coin with his face on it, if that's the case. But I'm just saying like all of this, it's like the White House. Everything is just white in the White House. You don't even got American Indians in the White House, or Latinos in the White House, or Chinese Americans in the White House. But it's all the White House and everything is like that. So y'all making all the decisions for us.

So it's not fair, man. And I feel bad for the white babies, for the Black babies, the Hispanic babies, the American Indian babies, because it's not their fault. They're coming into a world of shit right now, being born into it. They are being born into a world of shit where it's like, yo, it's going to be hard for them. It's going to be hard.

My ancestors used to get whipped, and the rest of the slaves had to sit out there and watch them get whipped until they died. When I watched George Floyd die, it felt like that. I felt like I was watching one of my relatives get whipped and get killed right in front of my face. And that got me angry. It's like I told my friends, better let your kids watch that so they can know what's going on in the world today.

To me, the new generation of white people, they cool. I think it's more the mothers and fathers of the generation of white people, like the old people that sit in the White House, and everybody old. They living off old traditions. So the newer ones are okay. I'm not going to say they're racist.

Like the fifties, the ones that's in the fifties and up and up, like, you know what I mean, sixties and seventies. When I look at the little twenty-five-year-old ladies and all that, they might get it from what they see, and get it from their parents and shit like that. I think the older ones, though, they seen it all. They was there since back then when King and Malcolm and all that. So it's already instilled in their hearts, like, these niggas are always going to be niggas. Whatever they want to call it. And that's it, they're ready to go. And that's why we still got these policemen. They still on the job because the police chief is not firing them, the sergeant ain't firing them. Because they come from that bloodline. It's a bloodline of cops like that.

And it's, like, I'm not saying every cop is crooked. I know there are nice cops out there. But a lot of them are abusing their power. Like they're going to jump a dude, but why it always has to be—and don't get it twisted, I'm not saying for it to be a white man or Chinese man—but why is y'all killing us Black people? And that's why at times I wish Malcolm X was still here. The ones that aren't putting up with it anymore.

Do you know how many times we put up with this shit? Getting sprayed with water hoses. Getting dogs set on us. Motherfuckers hanging us. Slaves, the slave masters was fucking our girls and doing all this other shit. It's, like, we never did that shit to the white people, man. And then when Black people start really wigging out for real, when they get on some fucking Black Panther shit around here and start just fucking everything up. Then we're the ones who are crazy.

I can't imagine how many people got killed without even a camera on them because of the justice system, our system, the government. I think it's going to take a lot of us to die. We're going to have to die for what's right. And it's sad, but you know what, if they still doing it, then the frontline troops got to come up. We got to just come out and die to stand for something. But the only thing is, like, if we do get on the front line and die, or are we going to still live it out and not turn pussy and fold and be like, "Oh, I don't want to do that now. I don't want to get violent because I got kids and I got this and I got that." No, we all got to go in and hold hands and go in as a struggle. Even if we got to hold hands and die together.

I'm going to tell the people now: If anything ever happened to me by fucking cops, don't march for me. Don't protest for me. You go out and you kill some motherfuckers, get busy. Because marching don't do nothing. All that marching and turn the other cheek. What are you going to do if somebody smacks you in the face a thousand times, and he continues to smack your face? You going to keep walking away a thousand times. No. You're going to swing back. Even if it's one time, you're going to swing back. You not going to be telling me if you got smacked and killed and all this other shit that you're just going to take it. It's like yo, no. These like the Martin Luther King days, no more man. These days is rough. It's rougher than the King days. King stirred some shit, don't get me wrong. You know, the dogs was on his ass, the FBI was watching him day and night, and all this other shit. But today, if you going to march, they don't give a fuck about a march.

Martin Luther King died for us to get freedom. He was like, "yo, listen man, this what we gonna do. I'm going to be the voice of it." And I respect him, because you know what? He died, I think at thirty-nine years old. He was a young dude when he was killed. He wasn't even forty yet. He could have been my son.

So it's like when he had that voice and they fucked around with it, which you might call the difference between him and Malcolm X, he wants to go to the nice way. But when you go the nice way, they motherfucking take advantage of you. They take advantage of you and that's what's happening. They killed his ass. And now you got Malcolm X. He's like, "no, fuck these motherfuckers. Let's go."

> "Because if you keep taking that ass whipping and not doing nothing about it, they going continue to whip y'all ass. But they got to stop doing it. They got to stop. I'm not promoting violence, but I am, like, 'I believe in an eye for an eye.'"

It's not fair since day 1. Since we was taken as slaves and brought over here. It wasn't fair. And I'm not saying all white people is bad and all that. Us as Black people, we probably had slaves ourselves. As far as Black slaves and shit, but we wouldn't go across the water. We wouldn't take somebody from their own land and bring them to fucking Africa and do all this other shit. Never did that shit. We was taken and stolen. And whether it was our own people that sold us into slavery and shit like that, that's still dealing with the dissatisfied within yourself.

For instance, America is not our land. You know what I mean? To be in your land . . . When I went to Africa, right? I had a connection. I had a connection because I felt so good to be there. Whether or not that was my birthplace. I don't think I was born in that part of town, maybe. But it was a connection there. It was like, you felt good spiritually. So it's like, how could you be connected to a land that you're not even from? Exactly. We're not from here. You know what I mean? That's why a lot of us probably have a lot of trouble and a lot to deal with because we're not connected to this earth here. Not the earth. We're not connected to America. You say I'm born African American. Listen, I'm African. Yeah. You know what I mean? I don't see Spanish American. Rastafarian American. Or Chinese American. Why you got to put the stand for me, African American. Why I can't just be African?

CHAPTER 15

TRIUMPH

Yo! Yo! Yo fuck that!
Look at all these crab niggas laid back
Lampin' like them gray and black Pumas on my man's rack
Codeine was forced in your drink
You had a navy green salamander fiend,
bitches overheard you scream
You two-faces scum of the slum, I got your whole body numb
Blowing like Shalamar in eighty-one
Sound convincing, thousand-dollar cork-pop convention
Hands like Sonny Liston, get fly permission
Hold the fuck up, I'll unfasten your wig, bad luck
I humiliate separate the English from the Dutch
It's me, black Noble Drew Ali
Came in threes we like the Genovese
Sazo, Caesar needs the greens
It's Earth ninety-three million miles from the first
Rough turbulence the wave burst, split the megahertz

I took something from all these guys and applied it to me. And they gave birth to a Ghostface. It's like they don't even know that, but I know that.

Cap had the most slang. Rae had fly shit. He knew a lot of fly words and fly this, though I applied these guys from the Clan style to my style. Dirty had the soul. I got my soul and not giving a fuck from Dirt. That's all Dirt, because I grew up off soul records. Dirt just made it come alive. He didn't give a fuck, just went ahead and did what he did. Meth had all the styles. RZA's like a fucking doctor. Genius is like a scientist. Deck got words. "I bomb atomically, Socrates philosophies . . ." It's like "Yo, this nigga's killing these crazy." He knew how to put his words together. It makes it sound like a real, real, real . . . like sound phat. He knew how to make your shit sound phat. Just random words. Sound phat, you've got to make your shit sound phat. Just words, random words. And Masta Killa's like a ninja. He's a ninja on tracks, because of the way he come in, it's just crazy.

But I took a lot of shit from all of them. I took everything that I know from all of them. I got a piece from here, a piece from here, a piece from here. It depends what pieces you use the most. And they made me great.

RZA had a vision. He carried out his vision in a smart way and brought all of us to where we were supposed to be. You have to respect that, regardless of

Ghostface and RZA on The Source, March 2000

what you go through. Sure, you're going to argue and have disagreements and stuff like that, but you can't take away from then to now. I don't give a fuck what you try to do. You got to look at yourself in the mirror and be like, "Okay, if it wasn't for this man that had that vision, would you be standing right here?"

I don't really got nothing bad to say about RZA like that. We had little discrepancies and differences and all that, but at the end of the day, I'm grateful for the steps he made and that he took me with him. Even though I was out there, busting my hump, doing what I had to do, it was like, okay, you know what, it's time. Because everything is about timing. If we wasn't around each other at that time, I don't know what would have happened. I don't know if he still could have moved on like that or I could've moved on and done something else as well.

But sometimes you need the right people in your circle to make things move. RZA and me could've done Wu-Tang on our own, but it wouldn't have been like the Wu-Tang right now because the rest of the group, everybody played their part to make Wu-Tang what it is, how the people see it. We wouldn't have had no big-ass cult probably if it was just me and RZA. So we needed these elements. We needed all of them to come together like that.

But he was the one that was pressing those buttons and getting up every night, every day, every morning, back and forth to the city and doing all this shit like that. He had the dream. It was his dream. That's what attracted me to him or him to me or whatever it was. But like I said, I just seen the light over him. My imagination is crazy, but you just see something about him was special that made you want to be around him and shit like that. So I know it was the light. The energy, his knowledge and wisdom. All of that. So he knows how to add things up, and then by the time the sum of it comes to him, he already knows what to do. Mathematics don't lie. But the way he adds and subtracts, it was beautiful. And that's why, at the end of the day, no member of Wu-Tang could ever really front on him. I don't care how mad you are. So that was that.

Even when I filed my lawsuit back in '05, that was just business. It was nothing personal. I don't want to blow it up all like that. I don't like putting our business in the street and shit, but we had the lawsuits. We just went to court, and it was business to be handled. I don't really want to go too deep into why, because I don't think it's everybody's business because it's family. That goes for anyone in the Clan. Even if you was my best friend, it's like what me and my best friend go through is just between us. It's not for everybody.

GZA is my brother. I love GZA. GZA and Ol' Dirty Bastard is cousins. Genius is the godfather. He showed me and everybody how to fucking rap.

There's something about having knowledge yourself. When you think the way certain people have knowledge, and the way they think, the way they speak, it goes into how they write the music, too. And Genius was always a wizard at that. He's an intelligent speaker.

Ghostface and GZA

I tell people he writes rhymes all day. I tell people Genius is the best rapper ever. He writes rhymes like the newspaper, he might run *The New York Times*. He's like a scientist. Him and RZA is like doctors and professors, because they can break down a rock and tell you the elements that's in a rock or in the wing of a bird or something. They know these things like that. And that's why I love his mind so much.

That's my brother right there. He was the one, he's so genuine and giving at the same time, it's, like, if anybody was to front on GZA, it'll have me ready to fuck around and just kill a motherfucker. Like, yo, don't play with him because he's special. Certain people you can't afford to—I'm not saying you could lose anybody, but there's some people that just can't lose.

Like all my brothers, I would go out for all of them. Even if you got me mad, I'm the type of person I'll still fight for you. And do anything. That's Genius. How he sees the world, how he sees shit is like looking through his eyes, it's another beautiful thing.

That's why I love to see him and RZA play chess. I like to see him and Masta Killa play chess. They all got different ways.

I love Masta Killa. I love his mind, too. They all beautiful minds. Because we all see each other, see things on the same wavelengths. Some brothers might have more knowledge and more insight on different things that they talking about and more. And me, I'm like a sponge. I soak it up. I listen. Even when they don't think I'm probably listening.

Masta Killa, he's like a silent killer. He's like a ninja. You might be in the room full of people, but you never hear him really walk up on you. Until he's right there, and tap you right on your shoulder. But his mind is just like RZA's and Genius's minds. Because when you can hear those three have a conversation and they build it, it gets deep. But their geekiness is beautiful to me, because it's like, I could see the minds working. We all are one mind.

When I can see it, I can comprehend it. Even if I can't speak it, I see it. So that's why I love when Masta Killa and Genius and RZA would play chess, or they building. Even a DJ, a lot of

Mathematics, same beautiful mind like that. All of them are like that. Those three brothers right there, its their breed there. They'll be loved.

Me and Raekwon, we match together. That's like a duo; as far as street shit, me and Rae know fly shit. I learned a lot of shit off the corner. The way Raekwon look at shit, it's like, "Hmm, I see it." Because we got pretty much the same mind when it comes to the streets. He knows

Raekwon and Ghostface

a lot of chunky, fly shit. And I like chunky, fly shit. And he knows how to put it together. He makes shit look cool. Rae wears size 9, every sneaker he put on his feet looked chunky to me, it looks fat. I get mad, because I'm a 13. I can't put them on them like he put them on. New Balance, Saucony, Asics—they all look crazy on his foot. The fresh pair, while it be sunny, his shit look crazy. The Timberlands and all that shit.

When me and Rae get together, people say we're Starsky and Hutch, Batman and Robin. It's shit like that. For his rap shit, Rae's in the zone for it, especially for the street takes. So me and Rae know that street shit. And we go together when we rap. As far as the streets, I'd rather run with him than anything. It's just a matter of being comfortable, at ease, and knowing that you guys are headed in the same direction—the minds are in sync, basically. You're on the same wavelength, I think, is what it comes down to.

Inspectah Deck is, like, he the inspector. Deck is one of them brothers that's right there. Like he made me laugh and shit, too. Mind you, all these motherfuckers is funny. They have you on the floor laughing like a motherfucker. Deck is a brother of peak shit. You can't really get nothing past Deck because he's smart. Like all these motherfuckers I'm talking about, they smart. And a good brother, we never hung out in the streets like that. But Deck could go out. Deck ain't no sucker. He going to go out with you.

Deck is the best lead-off man I've ever seen or heard in my life. He's always observing, that's why he's Inspectah Deck, because he's inspecting your conversation, even as you're spitting it, even your movements. And that's why we can laugh at it, because it'd be when he singing, it becomes like, "Yo, this motherfucker thought he was slick." He may tell you, "You didn't keep that? You didn't keep how we moved, and went over there, and this and that and the third?" That's Deck's prime for you right there. That's Deck.

And all my brothers is humble. They are humble. But we so wise now it's like you ain't going to just be able to get over on him like that because one thing that bothers me, they all know they keep gaining. They know when you're gaming them or you trying to spin a nigga. They know when you trying to spin them. So Deck is somebody to go out with you. I love Deck. He's quiet. He's quiet, and that's when he's in his quiet zone. I don't give a fuck if you think you doing something slick. He's peeping you, he knows what's what, and what's going on, always.

U-God. Poundcake, that's my man Poundcake right there. I call him Poundcake. Because poundcake is yellow with light skin, the outside of it. Almost like butter loaf. Golden, he golden.

But he's a fly dude, too. Now, Golden Arms is special. Especially when it comes to the wardrobes, he knows how to put his pieces together, too. He just looks good all the time. Him and Rae know how to make they clothes look good. These little-feet motherfuckers, they little-feet niggas. But they still look chunky, though.

I seen U-God with the gold front and also in the back of his mouth, but it looked fly though. And him as the MC, he got that voice. He got a deep Lou Rawls, deep-shit voice. It's strong. That's why he's an important element when it comes to the Clan, too.

I love U-God. Back in the days, we used to be all doing this shit when we was in the Wu mansions and shit out there in LA, arguing in the house over this and that. But it never got physical, and shit like that.

U-God is like, he's U-God. One minute he's like this, then one minute he's like that. Everything is a fuck with him. Oh, fuck that. Fuck that. They're going to fuck this

Triumph

shit. Fuck that, bro. Fuck, fuck, fuck. And it's like, I had to learn to grow with him. I had to learn to grow to be like, that's just him. That's just who he is.

But beautiful soul though. Beautiful soul. Because when you with him just having a one-on-one, a real heart-to-heart. Even if you say, "Oh, shit. Yo, you looking good right there. What you doing? You glowing right now." He's kind of spiritual, too. Because one day he came up on me when we were somewhere. He's like, "I see your wings. I see wings on you glowing, okay. I see wings on you." Well, you know, I had to laugh and shit. I don't see what he see. But he is a spiritual brother, he has his ways. Sometimes you don't know when to say hi or when not to say hi. So whenever we get into a disagreement, it's never like, "Yo, bro, I'm sorry." It's just like, I might pass him the mic on stage one day and that might start the conversation. "Yo, here take that, because I don't want you to go out with a fucked-up mic." So it's like, "Yo, here take this."

He might pass the mic back and be like, "All right, good luck." And now that we see each other in the halls or whatever, it might lead to a "What's up? Are you and the band downstairs? Or down there or not." And it's simple shit. But you know what? You got to have elements. And we all understand each other's power. We know what ticks a nigga off. We know who's humble. We know who's like, "Yo, you know what? If I say something to this nigga, he's going to spaz out." And it shit like that.

Like Rae, Rae don't give a fuck. Rae going to say what's on his chest. And fuck what everybody say, that's just Rae. Masta Killa's going to say what's on his chest. But he might hold it a little bit more longer. He might hold it a little bit longer and express it in a nice way. It depends on the current. It depends on the current that we in at that time, if it's a hot current. Or if it's a cold current. Did he go and come and let you have it, but it depends. But for the most part, those are the two that's really going to really say what's on they fucking mind and shit like that.

Now we got Cappadonna, he's the poppy-wardrobe king. Now it's not just U-God and Raekwon. Cap is like, he's poppy wardrobe. He can make anything look crazy. I don't give a fuck, if it's a button-up shirt with the half sleeves on it. He make his hat—the way he wears his hat will make that shirt look fly.

Ghostface and Cappadonna

Cappa come to you with gold fronts on his mouth, with a nice fucking little satellite dish chain on. Like, yo, and this shit is crazy. So that's Cap right there.

That's why, when you look at the "Triumph" video, he switched up to like twenty-one outfits in that shit. Twenty-one outfits in the mic check. That's one of his songs. So his wardrobe, the way he puts his shit together, too, it be looking dope on him. Like everybody got their own little unique shit about them.

I love Cap because Cap is the most on stage out of us all right now. Him and Meth are the best motherfuckers on the stage. They're going to give it a hundred every time. Everybody give it a hundred, but it's how you go. It's how you give it, and the way Cap and Meth give up the hundred, nobody can give it up like how they give it up.

Cappadonna and Ghostface

Meth'll freestyle, Cap'll freestyle anywhere. Write his thoughts. Good brother. Good brothers playing. Cap brought a lot of slang to the town. So his slang is off the hook. Like "Spock that pepper." "Where that broccoli at?" All that's weed. He the one that introduce me to pink toes when he was like, "Yo, look at the pink toes." It was a white chick, though. He was like, "Yo, man, I might slay me some pink toes," or something.

But I got it. I caught on. I caught on a little bit after, because he come with so many angles. You come at so many angles because the slang is like, he's a slang therapist. He'd be like, "Where that booger foot? I go for that best, like that booger green. That's like that booger green that's like that weed. Yo, who got that booger foot?" Come on, man. He do his own shit. He the only motherfucker that could walk the streets of Chicago by himself, and then take the bus to wherever he's going to get on a bus and come back. Like five in the morning. Be in your hood. Cap'll be in your hood at five in the morning. Nigga be in the projects in Queens and fall rocks somewhere at four, five in the morning, sitting on the bench, and come back. He's one of those. Easy, you know? Yeah. He's Crazy Eddie right now.

He'll just want to check the scene. He wound up in the hood party for dolo. But he still go to the hoods, though, and break bread. Many times me and him done spend a thousand dollars in 7-Eleven and gave it to the homeless right outside the building. Gave to fifty people out there like that. And shit like this. It's like, "Yo, we going to go up in there, buy a thousand dollars' worth of shit and just give you motherfuckers mad juice, mad bread, mad waters." Whatever they need. And we did that many times. Like, yo, just speak whatever's on the bus. We'll go out and feed the people. We'll park the bus right here. Look at them homeless right there. Yo, give them whatever's on the bus and give it to the people, feed them. That's Cap. That's Cappadonna for you right there.

Then you got the great Method Man. There were times I went broke, Meth lent me money back in the day. Back in '94–'95, I was like, "Yo, I need this, let me get five Gs, yo, Method. Got to pay my rent, and this and that." Because I was blowing money at the time. I didn't know how to control my money. Meth was out there doing his thing. He coughed up that shit and gave it to me with no questions asked. He just was like, "Yo," and wrote the check. I could never front on Meth. Never, ever, ever, ever, ever front on Meth like that—that's my brother right there.

Meth had the hoods. Meth had the hoods buzzing back then, too. Because he had mad styles. He had like thirty-six styles. That's why we chose him to go first over that Wu-Tang shit. He had mad style. And he choked that Method Man shit. And you know, he choked it so bad. He would always tell us that me and Rae took him out of his zone. Because we used to play around with him. We were just fucking with him, but Meth took it to heart. Because I'd be like, "Yo, why you don't back into that Method Man shit?" Yo, he said, "No, you already fucked me up." I feel bad for that. Because, we liked to snap back then and fuck around with just about anybody.

Meth's style is so ill, he was blowing all of us away. First of all, I wasn't even on that level, like that. But he was blowing us out. Like me and Rae, with his styles and shit, like that. Blowing us completely out the frame. That's why everybody took a liking to Method Man in the beginning. That's why when I say, on "Cherchez LaGhost," the first lines: "Brothers try to pass me, but none could match me. / No girl can freak me, I'm just too nasty."

"That's four bars from Method Man off one of the tapes he did back in the day. I took that from Meth from back then, put it on *Supreme Clientele*, because I just liked how it sounded."

But Meth is a good nigga. Everybody loves Meth. He's like the Michael Jackson of the clique. He holds so much weight, when he don't show up, it's liable to feel it. That's why I be so glad when he shows up at important shit. He'd be busy doing movies. But when he shows up, he shows up. And I could look at him and I could tell him, like, "Yo, tell these niggas got to move around, they not dancing. We got to move, niggas, we a group. We look stupid just standing in one spot." Meth will go there, and tell niggas in there, "Move around." If you out there by yourself, say I'm rocking on stage, I got that mic, I'm doing "Ice Cream," Meth will come over there, and he'll rock with me on it. Or rock with me on certain verses that I do. He'd come in and help me out, to make it look like, okay, we in sync as a team. But when other people would get on stage and do it, a lot of times, some of the times, not all the time, but some of the times, people were not in sync. But Meth would come and be like, "Hey. Get that. Get that. Get that." And bring it to you like that.

He could make you fall in. But I could be there already, I might just be worried about my other brothers. Because I know how I like to look on stage. But do everybody else know how they look? I know how we should look on stage. It just takes teamwork to put that big-ass stage show together. Right wardrobes, the right props, the right shit. I like my shit looking like a play. It'll look like a play on stage. But sometimes we ain't moving with all that shit, we just got our talent and our records to speak for us. So we got to try to paint that picture the most way we could paint it.

> "And Meth's a master on that stage, because he was going out before all of us. He was going out on them little blackout shows that Jay-Z ran when Jay-Z had his 'Hard Knock Life' tours, and all that other shit. Meth, he was out there. Then when him and Redman got together, it was lights-out. It was over."

Meth likes perfection. He likes it like that, though. He's different, though, because certain shit Meth like, I don't like. It's like that sometimes. You ain't going to like what everybody like. But he puts that work in on a stage. If it was based on how much you sweated your shirt out? Like how much sweat you perspire, I might come in third place every night. But I know Method got first or second. Every night. Some nights, if my sugars fucking with me and shit, it depends, I might come in last. It was a couple of times I came in last. I didn't leave the stage with my shirt wet. I ain't put that much work in. Putting that work in just moving around. Moving around. Just moving around doing shit. Because you ain't going to sweat standing like that. But that's me and my own shit. My sugar could have went low a few times on stage. That shit make you weak. Because that's the only time they fuck with me, make sure I got orange juice there, got my insulin, and shit like that.

But I get through it because I got my brothers there. And they're going to do what they do until my shit come back. And then, all right, I'll just jump in in a minute. I'll take it easy. I'll do my verse and play the back or something. But yeah man, we know, and if you don't sweat and come out like that, maybe just showing a little bit of sweat, that means you ain't really putting that much work in.

And Meth would go out. Meth ain't no sucker. He don't fuck around. And he ain't no troublemaker. But if you see you getting into some shit, and he's there like that, and he see it, somebody going to get laid out.

ODB. That was like another brother to me right there. Dirt was like . . . his name was Ason Unique. So he was unique in every way.

First time I met him, he didn't even know me, he just asked me for a piece of my hero pastrami sandwich. Straight up, "Yo, let me get a piece of that right there. Yo, that looks banging and shit. Can I get a piece of that?" Again, this is the first time I ever met him. So, I broke him off a half. "Yo, word to my babies, that's the best sandwich I ever had."

Everything was "Word to the babies, word to my babies. The best sandwich I ever had. That's the best shit I tasted. Where's the phone? Where's the phone." I began to love this motherfucker deeply, deeply. We drank together. Did everything. He's the one that really gave me all my soul. He gave me soul. We didn't give a fuck. Just didn't give a fuck about nothing, because it's going to be what it's going to be. That's why we always said, "God made Dirt. Dirt don't hurt."

He'd drop his sandwich on the floor and wipe it off. Pick it up, wipe it off, eat it. He was one of those, brah. I've seen him walk up on females and be like, he trying to talk to them, but be like, "Yo, you don't know who I am? You don't know who I am?" Then sing a song: "Me Mariah, go back like babies and pacifiers, Old Dirt Dog . . ."

And the girl . . . I'm looking, I'm laughing. This nigga got to be crazy. Because the chick ain't know who he was, he going to sing his fucking song. And then go bag the chick, get the chick. Before you know what, she at the hotel or the fucking show. I've seen him run up on chicks like, "Yo, baby, I'll kiss you, I'll put my tongue in your mouth right now. As word to my babies, I'll tongue you down right now. Right now." We could be in the mall. He'd say whatever, "You sexy chocolate motherfuckers. These chocolate motherfuckers, sexy . . ." But she can't even get mad because he's complimenting her at the same time.

I'm waiting for the smack to come, and this nigga never got smacked. I never seen nobody do what he did. He'd come in a hotel with fifty women. I seen it one day in Philly, with like fifty women and just be like, "Yo, Ghost, you all right? Yo, you all right? You and Rae, you all right?

You all right? You all right?" And we had other people around us. He asked them is they all right. Everybody taking a chick. Everybody like, "Yo!"

This is in the beginning days, like in '93, '94. Yeah. Like, "Here, you go with him." He was saying shit like, "You go with him. You go with him." We had them all. I never seen nobody like him. Nobody.

He was funny, though. I remember one day I had to laugh. I was out of state somewhere. I was in Ohio, and he came through. My man gave him some sneakers. And they was LA Gears. Now, I looked at this nigga's feet, he got them LA Gears on, I start dying laughing. He has LA Gears on. And he looked down at his feet and he had to laugh. He busted up, but he tried to match the LA Gears because they was purple and black, and he had a purple shirt on. So he tried to match the LA Gears with his shirt. I'm dying laughing, yo, mega hard. Like, "Yo, nigga, you's a fool." I'm on the floor. "All right. Stop. Chill, chill, chill." He was the same way. Because he knew them LA Gears was some whack-ass sneakers. But he didn't give a fuck, because he was out of town and then niggas was slow out. He didn't really give a fuck back then. They was slow. But it was LA Gears. I died laughing.

> "He used to get drunk. He used to go to my house with my mother and my aunt alone, he'd be in the kitchen, singing, 'I hope that we can be together soon.' All that shit like that from Teddy Pendergrass. My mother, she'd get drunk and she'd sing, too."

My brother's in a wheelchair, but the other brothers, he was dying, laughing. Darius, he's in a wheelchair, he laughed, and they got the whole house rolling. They got the whole house rolling. My other brothers, me, and Dirt went to Queens, to Roosevelt Island, somewhere like that. And we checked on my brother Devon in the hospital. And I play "Protect Ya Neck" for my brother, and he liked it. When he got to Ol' Dirty Bastard's part, he started smiling. He started laughing. Because right after that, my brother Devon passed away. My first brother, right after me. He heard Ol' Dirty's voice, that's when I knew Dirt was special, because my brothers and them, they think how I think, so it's like, when he got to him, when he got to Dirty's, "First thing first," my brother, yo, he had that smile. He's lying on his bed. He had that smile on his face. It reached him. And I know they would have loved Ol' Dirt. He would have been a fan of Ol' Dirt, straight up, because Dirt liked everybody. And everybody on "Protect Ya Neck," the way Dirt's style was on that one, he stood out a lot.

Dirt was just like . . . he was just Dirt, man. We stole shit from the store. I seen the liquor store man shooting at him one day. He stole a bottle out the liquor store, with the man from the store shooting at him. Running up the block and still got the bottle. The first man I ever seen on national TV with his kids and his girl, go cash his check, get the food stamps. Got food stamps on TV. They didn't go ahead and go bust it down. He went over there and just fucked around on them. Yo, he went to the store and bust the food stands down and got cash. That's what he do. And he was getting money, and he was still getting money. So it was rent money. He's getting rent money. Nigga tell me, "All money is good money. I don't give a fuck, it's money."

He brought that same energy up on stage. And I just see Dirt. To me, Dirt was like, "Meth's killing it." I used to think Dirt didn't like that because he wanted all the fans. So I'll be on the side of Dirt, and I see Dirt shaking his leg, tapping his feet on the floor like that. But he's watching Meth on stage and the crowd going crazy for Meth. Now, Dirt got to be next to go on. That nigga, he always would think of something. He'd walk out there and just stand there and look at the crowd. Not say nothing. And the crowd would just erupt. At the time, when I looked at it from there, I ain't going to tell nobody that shit, it was like a battle for the crowd. It could be like a battle. Even if somebody did some stupid, he'd look at me with that smile. And I already know what it is, because Dirt thinking bullshit, or Dirt just think that he's frightened, or whatever the case may be.

You would know what he was thinking about. Meth will be on, and I'm right there next to him. They're not going to look at him, shaking his leg. Not all the time, he won't look at me, but I knew. I could tell. Because I know him, I know him. We had personal conversations. We lived next to each other. He used to look at me, and I already know what he's thinking and shit. And he'd just go, and he'd turn up.

Ol' Dirty Bastard N***a Please *cassette*

But he'd fuck around and look and then go walk out there. Because he seen Meth killing it, like murder it. Then Dirt got to do something to top that shit. And this nigga is good. He'd do the Ason. His Ason dance was loud. Nobody could do the Ason like Dirt could. He had his own dance. So he out there, taking the shirt off. Doing shit.

He was just off the meet, right? He didn't give a fuck. Yeah. How's he going to go up on the Grammys and be like, "I went out and bought an outfit today that costed a lot of money, you know, because I figured Wu-Tang was gonna win." How are you going to go up there and say that? "I don't know how y'all see it, but when it comes to Wu-Tang, Wu-Tang is for the children, we teach the children, you know what I mean?" He looked at Erykah (Badu). "Puffy is good, but Wu-Tang's the best. Peace."

And they was trying to take him off the stage. How are you going to do that? He was special. He's special. He's the cousin of RZA and Genius. That whole thing, right there. They was the "All in Together [Now]" crew. That was them right there.

I also did a couple of small things for film. I did *Belly* in 1998, that was a cameo. Then there was *Black and White* in 1999. That was the Cream Team, with Method Man, Raekwon, Masta Killa, Inspectah Deck, and Power. It was the one with Mike Tyson and then all that. And, again, I just had a cameo.

Yeah. I was supposed to appear in the movie *Iron Man*, but because they didn't use that scene, it got in the deleted scenes. But when he first saw me . . . I didn't even know he knew me. He said, "You the real Tony Stark." I was just more happy for him knowing me. It wasn't even a lot of people when he approached me, I think he might have been going to his trailer, and I'm coming out of the trailer trying to go to the thing, and he just . . . We just both bumped into each other, "Yo, what up. Yeah, you're the real Tony Stark." He let me borrow his private jet in Dubai, and I sent for some girls. I sent them some girls like, "Yo, you go with him." And he's like, "Yo, I need my jet." I said, "Yo, when you need the jet back?"

So that was that. And I did *30 Rock*. I was up there a little bit, a couple of times, trying to learn some lines, and I was in *The Dewey Cox Story*, I don't even remember what the fuck I did in there. And then *When in Rome*, that was a fucking nightmare, because I had to do my lines like a hundred times in front of like a hundred people. And I was embarrassed for that, because I couldn't learn my line. And it wasn't even a big line, but it was like curator, it was something, something dealing with curator. And I couldn't say the word curator, so it was like, then I'm saying it backward, like saying it first. It was just . . . it was too much. I was really, really embarrassed in front of all the people there. And I know, I'm like, "Oh, shit. What the fuck. Why I can't get it?" I'll never let that happen again. But, they never . . . I don't even think they gave me the lines, the script, so I could learn that shit. I had to get there, and they were like, "Okay, there's your line right here. This is your line, this is what you're going to say." It was one of those, and I couldn't say the shit. So I've been like a hundred times embarrassed. I did a couple of things, writing like that, or whatever.

> "The *Mob Wives*, that one was filmed on Staten Island, so that's my peoples. My manager hooked it up. All I did was a little cameo in there too, a little scene, and that was it."

People say I got a different, I don't know, I guess it's a different swagger or whatever. I don't like using the word "swagger," but my demeanor is different, and people always me telling me like, "Yo, you should go act, yo." I remember when I first met Big Daddy Kane, he told me that one day, too. He might've been the first one to tell me like, "Yo, you should go for acting and shit." I guess he might've seen something, or whatever. But I heard that from a lot of people, even my friends and all that. I guess they could just see me in it.

I look back on everything, I put in a lot of work over the years: thirteen solo albums, seven Wu-Tang albums, and eleven more albums with artists I consider close family like D-Block, Wu Massacre (Meth and Raekwon), Theodore Unit, Czarface, and others. Over fifteen of those debuted in the Billboard Top 10—that's a hell of a catalog, a lot of beats, ink, and paper. Classics. But I'm still in the studio churning out music. I got an unreleased album with MF Doom out there, *Supreme Clientele 2* in the can and ready to blow, and the Clan has at least one more joint in us we wanna give the world.

Overall, life is good—right now I'm all about staying healthy, staying in shape so I can keep rocking that stage as long as possible. I am blessed right now, we the Rolling Stones of this hip-hop shit. What group you know been together over twenty-five years and still touring and putting out relevant music . . . nobody!

I go out on the road on average about two hundred shows a year, fifty to sixty of those with the Clan, the rest on my own. Over the years, the fan base has gotten bigger and bigger, seems like more and more people coming out to see us. I look at the makeup of the crowds—we be having fifty-year-old grannies all the way down to kids who are barely teenagers. It's like four or five generations of Wu-Tang fans out here for us. It's our music—it's timeless. It's music for the children. It never gets old. Every generation need them jewels and the knowledge in those records. It's passed on from the OGs to they grandkids, you know what I'm sayin'?

There ain't nothing like that energy you get when you connecting with the fans at a show, running through joints, hearing them singing along, DJ drops the record, and the entire building is finishing my verse for me. That's real shit right there, legendary shit, so I give my fans everything I got every show. I leave it all on that stage every night. Blood, sweat, and tears, it don't matter how I'm feeling. Sometimes my diabetes got me feeling low. You know long flights, especially going to Europe, for a diabetic are no good, but I thug through it, drink some OJ, take my vitamins. I suck it up for the fans—they don't see it, but I go through a lot of shit to be there for them . . . 'cause they there for me . . . it's a bond we share that will never go away.

PHOTO CREDITS

Cover photo by Craig Wetherby
Page 5 Photo furnished by Mike Caruso
Page 7 Photo furnished by Mike Caruso
Page 21 Photo furnished by Mike Caruso (Ghost & UN)
Page 29-32 Illustrations by Nate Reilly
Page 38 Photo by Craig Wetherby
Page 50 Photo by Craig Wetherby
Page 33 Photo furnished by Mike Caruso
Page 54 Photo furnished by Mike Caruso
         (Ghost on Stairs)
Page 55 Photo by Johnny Nunez (Ghost w/ Cola tee)
Page 55 Photo by Craig Wetherby
Page 56 Photo by Johnny Nunez
Page 57 Photo by Johnny Nunez (Ghost+Jadakiss)
Page 59 Photo by Johnny Nunez (Ghost+RZA)
Page 61 Photo by Craig Wetherby (Ghost in Tokyo)
Page 64 Photos furnished by Mike Caruso
Page 66 Photo by Johnny Nunez (Ghost, Deck & Rifkind)
Page 79 Photo furnished by Mike Caruso
         (Wu Gambino items)
Page 81 Photo furnished by Mike Caruso
Page 87 Photo by Craig Wetherby (Ghost Oxygen)
Page 91 Photos furnished by Mike Caruso
Page 96 Photo by Johnny Nunez (Ghost Atlas)
Page 97 Photos furnished by Mike Caruso

Page 100 Photo by Johnny Nunez
         (Hot97 Ghost Atlas + Ghost ring)
Page 114 Photo furnished by Mike Caruso
Page 117 Photos furnished by Mike Caruso
Page 119 Photo by Craig Wetherby (Ghost Notebooks)
Page 127 Photo by Craig Wetherby
         (Ghost Crowd Mexico City)
Page 128 Photo by Craig Wetherby
         (Ghost Notebook pages)
Page 134 Rage against the Machine Tour Poster
Page 135 Photo by Craig Wetherby (ghost/live)
Page 136 Photo by Craig Wetherby (Ghost w/ Mask)
Page 137 Photo by Craig Wetherby (WuFlag)
Page 139 Photo by Fulani Jabri
         (Ghost w/ Wutang in MGM)
Page 140 Photo by Craig Wetherby
         (Ghost in Kyoto w/map)
Page 140 Photo by Craig Wetherby
         (Ghost on Bullet Train/Japan 2007)
Page 142 Photo by Fulani Jabri (Young Dirty splits)
Page 142 Photo by Domingo Neris (NYSM tour tickets)
Page 143 Photo by Johnny Nunez
         (live on stage NYC bb king's)
Page 145 Photos furnished by Mike Caruso
Page 146 Photos furnished by Mike Caruso

Page 155 Photos furnished by Mike Caruso
Page 155 Photo by Johnny Nunez (Ghost+Jadakiss)
Page 159 Photo by Johnny Nunez (Ghost + Andre 3000)
Page 160 Photo furnished by Mike Caruso
Page 161 Photo furnished by Mike Caruso
Page 162 Photos furnished by Mike Caruso
Page 170 Doomstarks flyer furnished by
       Domingo Neris drawn by ArturoDraws
Page 173 Photos furnished by Mike Caruso
Page 174 Photos furnished by Mike Caruso
Page 176 Photo by Johnny Nunez (ghost+ redman)
Page 180 Photo by Johnny Nunez (Kevin Liles)
Page 181 Photo by Johnny Nunez (Ghost w/ Jay Z)
Page 182 Photo furnished by Mike Caruso
Page 183 Photo furnished by Mike Caruso
       (Marc Ecko watch)
Page 184 Photo by Craig Wetherby (Ghost in Iceland)
Page 185 Photos furnished by Mike Caruso (Collectibles)
Page 188 Photo by Johnny Nunez
       (Angie Martinez + Miss Info)

Page 190 Photo by Craig Wetherby
       (ghost/live/Mexico City)
Page 194 Photo furnished by Mike Caruso
Page 213 Photo furnished by Mike Caruso
Page 219 Photo furnished by Mike Caruso
       (Source Cover/March 2000)
Page 221 Photo by Johnny Nunez (Ghost + GZA)
Page 223 Photo by Johnny Nunez (Ghost + Rae)
Page 224 Photo by Fulani Jabri (Ghost + Goldie)
Page 227 Photo by Craig Wetherby (Ghost + Cap)
Page 228 Photo by Craig Wetherby (Ghost + Cap in studio)
Page 231 Photo by Johnny Nunez (Method Man)
Page 234 Photo by Bob Berg (Ghost & ODB)
Page 239 Photo by UGOD furnished by
       Domingo Neris (Crowd)
Page 234 Photo by Fulani Jabri
       (Ghost Live rocking MGM in Atlanta)